TEACHER EDUCATION
PARTNERSHIPS

Policy and practice

Critical Guides for
Teacher Educators

You might also like the following books in this series from Critical Publishing.

Ability Grouping in Primary Schools: Case Studies and Critical Debates
Rachel Marks
978-1-910391-24-2

Beginning Teachers' Learning: Making Experience Count
Katharine Burn, Hazel Hagger and Trevor Mutton
978-1-910391-17-4

Coteaching in Teacher Education: Innovative Pedagogy for Excellence
Colette Murphy
978-1-910391-82-2

Developing Creative and Critical Educational Practitioners
Victoria Door
978-1-909682-37-5

Developing Outstanding Practice in School-based Teacher Education
Edited by Kim Jones and Elizabeth White
978-1-909682-41-2

Evidence-based Teaching in Primary Education
Edited by Val Poultney
978-1-911196-46-3

Tackling Social Disadvantage through Teacher Education
Ian Thompson
978-1-912096-61-9

Teacher Educators in the Twenty-first Century: Identity, Knowledge and Research
Gerry Czerniawski
978-1-912096-53-4

Teacher Status and Professional Learning: The Place Model
Linda Clarke
978-1-910391-46-4

Theories of Professional Learning
Carey Philpott
978-1-909682-33-7

Our titles are also available in a range of electronic formats. To order please go to our website www.criticalpublishing.com or contact our distributor NBN International by telephoning 01752 202301 or emailing orders@nbninternational.com.

TEACHER EDUCATION
PARTNERSHIPS

Policy and practice

Series Editor: Ian Menter

Trevor **Mutton**
Katharine **Burn**
Hazel **Hagger**
Kate **Thirlwall**

First published in 2018 by Critical Publishing Ltd

British Library Cataloguing in Publication Data
A CIP record for this book is available from the British Library

ISBN: 9781912096572

This book is also available in the following e-book formats:
MOBI: 9781912096565
EPUB: 9781912096558
Adobe e-book reader: 9781912096541

Cover and text design by Greensplash Limited
Project Management by Out of House Publishing
Typeset by Out of House Publishing
Printed and bound in Great Britain by 4edge, Essex

Critical Publishing
3 Connaught Road
St Albans
AL3 5RX

www.criticalpublishing.com

Paper from responsible sources

CONTENTS

ABOUT THE SERIES EDITOR

Ian Menter is Emeritus Professor of Teacher Education and was formerly the Director of Professional Programmes in the Department of Education at the University of Oxford. He previously worked at the Universities of Glasgow, the West of Scotland, London Metropolitan, the West of England and Gloucestershire. Before that he was a primary school teacher in Bristol, England. His most recent publications include *A Companion to Research in Teacher Education* (edited with Michael Peters and Bronwen Cowie) and *Learning to Teach in England and the United States* (Tatto, Burn, Menter, Mutton and Thompson). His work has also been published in many academic journals.

ABOUT THE AUTHORS

Katharine Burn is an Associate Professor of Education at the University of Oxford and Director of the Oxford Education Deanery, a partnership between the university and local schools, encompassing the three strands of initial teacher education, continuing professional development and research. Her research interests span history education and teachers' professional learning at all career stages.

Hazel Hagger worked in secondary schools for a number of years before joining the University of Oxford to contribute to the development of one of the first initial teacher education (ITE) partnerships. She later became Director of Graduate Professional Courses. She has been involved in partnership development in a number of countries and has written extensively on teachers' learning and development.

Trevor Mutton is the current PGCE Course Director at the University of Oxford where he also contributes to the Masters programme in learning and teaching. He taught modern foreign languages before joining the university and has since been involved in a range of research into language teaching and into the nature of beginning teachers' learning, including the developing expertise of beginning teachers (DEBT) project.

Kate Thirlwall works at a large secondary school and is the current Senior Trainer for the SCITT programme based at her school, delivering training for School Direct initial teacher training programmes. Alongside this role, she works as an accredited Wellbeing Coach offering bespoke support to allow beginning teachers to reach their potential. Kate holds an MSc in Learning and Teaching from the University of Oxford. Her subject specialism is Modern Foreign Languages.

FOREWORD

Partnership is an enduring theme in teacher education in this country and around the world. Throughout the twentieth century it became increasingly apparent that the best teacher education was dependent on effective working relationships between schools and institutions of higher education. In England this was not officially recognised until the early 1990s when the government introduced requirements for teacher education providers that there should be a formal arrangement ensuring that the contributions of schools and their teachers were acknowledged.

However, the authors of this volume have worked in a partnership programme that had been developed and established before then, in the 1980s, which became known as the Oxford Internship Scheme (OIS). The OIS has continued to flourish since that time and has been a model for many other providers to learn from.

One of the authors of this text, Trevor Mutton, previously wrote about the concept of partnership insisting that it needs to be understood as a pedagogical term, as well as conveying the formal contractual relationships between universities and schools (Mutton, chapter 12 in Teacher Education Group, 2016). Previous work by one of his colleagues here, Hazel Hagger, together with the inspirational figure of the late Donald McIntyre, showed the power of the concept of *practical theorising* in teacher education (Hagger and McIntyre, 2006).

Mutton, Hagger and their colleague Katharine Burn also contributed an earlier volume in this series, called *Beginning Teachers' Learning: Making Experience Count* (Burn et al, 2015), in which they set out the lessons of their long-term research project, Developing Expertise of Beginning Teachers.

I myself was also fortunate to collaborate with Burn, Mutton and other colleagues in carrying out a comparative study in England and the United States, which examined in some depth developments in teacher education policy and practice that are currently occurring on either side of the Atlantic (Tatto et al, 2018).

The present volume builds on all of these prior experiences and presents a fascinating research-based account of partnership in practice – what it can mean and what it can achieve. The project on which the book is based was developed in collaboration with a school-based colleague, Kate Thirlwall, a collaboration that represents the research dimension of such relationships.

It is my belief that *Teacher Education Partnerships: Policy and Practice* represents a most significant contribution to our understanding of high-quality teacher education, not only in England, but globally.

Ian Menter, Series Editor
Emeritus Professor of Teacher Education, University of Oxford

CRITICAL **ISSUES**

- *What has been the role of partnership in the development of initial teacher education (ITE) policy over the past three decades?*
- *What are the pedagogical underpinnings of effective ITE partnerships?*

Introduction

Partnership working lies at the heart of teacher education, but there is no one model that fits all contexts. Different conceptualisations of partnership continue to evolve in a rapidly changing policy climate, both here in England and in other countries across the world. The purpose of this book is to examine the nature of ITE partnership working and to highlight some of the critical issues that those involved in such partnerships might need to address at both a practical and a conceptual level. The central part of the book is based around a case study of a school that is working simultaneously within two distinct ITE partnerships – a long-standing partnership with a university provider and a recently developed School Centred Initial Teacher Training (SCITT) programme based at the school itself. This provides an insight into the way that partnership working is evolving, particularly following the signifi-cant policy reforms that have taken place in England in recent years. Partnership has also been a central feature of various reviews of teacher education that have taken place over the last decade across the other jurisdictions of the United Kingdom, but in these analyses the focus has been '*more on partnership as the context for beginning teachers' learning*' (Mutton, 2016, p 209) and less on the logistical or structural aspects, as has been arguably the case in England. The significant reforms to teacher education policy which have taken place in this country have undoubtedly had at their heart an unquestioned acceptance of the importance of partnership working, be it within more traditional approaches or in what have been designated as 'school-led' models, but the emphasis has been predominantly on the structural relationships within these partnerships. For example, the government's promotion of 'school-led' models has carried with it very particular implications about the nature or balance of the partnership, where schools are expected to

take greater responsibility in the system. As employers of newly qualified teachers, schools have a critical interest in ensuring that they are of high quality and ready to teach and that new teachers are committed to teaching and intend to stay in the profession. They should play a greater role in recruitment and selection of new teachers; and over time, they should take on greater responsibility for managing the system.

(DfE, 2011a, p 14)

As this extract makes clear, underpinning these new approaches to teacher education at a national level is a serious policy concern about the nation's capacity to produce (and retain) high-quality teachers, capable of delivering the pupil outcomes necessary to improve the country's position in international 'league tables', such as the Programme for International Student Assessment (PISA) and the Trends in International Mathematics and Science Study (TIMSS). England is not alone in identifying this link between an adequate supply of high-quality teachers and high-quality pupil outcomes; concern about educational outcomes is widely associated with concern about the quality of teacher education (OECD, 2005, 2007; Schleicher, 2011). The above extract also highlights, however, that there are two separate but related issues – one concerning quality and the other concerning supply. The first focuses on the professional preparation of beginning teachers and raises questions as to what sort of preparation this entails and who can provide it most effectively; the second focuses on how sufficient numbers of people can be attracted into the teaching profession in order to meet current and future levels of need. These are separate policy questions which may have different answers; or it may be judged that the answers to one should over-ride the answers to the other. In both cases, however, effective forms of ITE partnership are seen as being central.

Teacher education partnerships matter and, as Bills et al (2008) concluded, in their systematic review of the literature on international perspectives on quality in ITE,

there is widespread agreement that effective school experience, and by extension the strength of the partnership between the provider and the schools, is central to the quality of initial teacher education.

(2008, p 14)

Any attempt at defining the term, however, leads immediately to a sense of the underlying complexity of the issues involved. Brisard et al (2005) began their extensive review of international models of partnership by suggesting that there were two conceptualisations of the term as it is used in the context of ITE, each with its accompanying literature:

First, there is the use of the term partnership to carry certain theories about the nature of learning to become a teacher. These theoretical precepts concern the pedagogy and curriculum of ITE. Second, though – and this logically does take second place – there are the uses of the term to describe particular arrangements for the delivery of ITE. These logistical concerns include such matters as the resourcing of initial teacher education, particular balances of responsibility between different roles or the placing of and arrangements for particular forms of school experience.

(2005, p 5)

In the rest of this chapter we trace the way in which these two conceptualisations of partnership have developed and examine the underlying issues in order to gain a better understanding of the nature of both policy and practice.

The evolution of policy

We begin by providing a brief overview of the development of teacher education policy in England over the past three decades, particularly as it relates to partnership working, in order to set current policies and practices in their historical context. The overview will focus on the way in which such development has taken place in England, as a specific case, but will also relate this to similar trends internationally, notwithstanding understandable differences in individual policy contexts.

Ever since training colleges first began to play a role in teacher education, there have been arrangements between universities and schools to accommodate the need for student teachers to gain some practical experience of the classroom. It was not, however, until the first wave of government reforms of teacher education in England in the early 1980s that partnership began to emerge as a central policy issue (see Furlong et al, 2000 and Brisard et al, 2005 for more detail of these developments). It was government circular 3/84 (DES, 1984) that set out for the first time requirements concerning the length of ITE programmes and the proportion of time to be spent in schools, but writing just ahead of these reforms Alexander (1984) was already identifying key issues around partnership work and highlighting the fact that differing conceptions of approaches to professional learning, held by universities and schools respectively, made the dialogue of partnership 'difficult to promote'. Furthermore he warned that the 'comfortable language of partnership', so easily adopted by policy-makers and others, could conceal 'more intractable issues' (1984, p 142).

Subsequent intervention by government, through Circulars 9/92 and 14/93 (DFE, 1992, 1993), made it a requirement that teacher education providers should enter into formal partnership arrangements with schools. The overwhelmingly positive responses to partnership development in the research literature of the period (Smedley, 2001) accompanied recognition of the valuable role to be played by classroom teachers in teacher education programmes, but while the statutory requirements meant that all providers would be engaging with partnership working in some form or another it could be argued that the 'rhetorical power of partnership' (Conroy et al, 2013, p 558) continued to mask further the 'intractable issues' to which Alexander had referred.

Under the 1997–2010 Labour government the approach to ITE partnership took on a new emphasis in 2001 with the National Partnership Project, introduced by the Teacher Training Agency (TTA), the funding agency for initial teacher training that had been set up by the previous government in 1994. The project had two aims – first, to increase capacity within the existing system so that more teachers could be trained, and, second, to improve the quality of that training. Generous funding was made available so that regional initiatives could be developed, many of which involved newly designated Partnership Promotion Schools working in conjunction with ITE providers, often around a mutually agreed on project. The way in which such cooperation took place was identified as a benefit of the project, which also succeeded in securing more school placements in some regions, but the national evaluation of the project found that it had done little to change underlying partnership practices (Furlong et al, 2006) and had actually undermined the *'pedagogical and epistemological dimensions of partnership'* in favour of a *'technical rationalist approach to teacher education'* (p 32), driven by market forces. These *'pedagogical and epistemological dimensions'* remind us of the *'theoretical precepts'* concerning *'the pedagogy and curriculum of ITE'* (Brisard et al, 2005) cited earlier, which will be explored more fully in subsequent sections of this chapter.

Partnership has remained at the heart of teacher education policy with further significant reform during the period of the Coalition government in 2010 and the continuation of those policies under subsequent Conservative governments. The introduction of School Direct was accompanied by a significant increase in the number of accredited School Centred Initial Teacher Training (SCITT) providers. SCITTs are led by groups of schools and colleges and are accredited initial teacher training providers in their own right, with all offering programmes leading to Qualified Teacher Status (QTS). Many also work in conjunction with a university to award a Postgraduate Certificate in Education (PGCE). Two significant policy documents in 2011 (DfE, 2011a, 2011b) gave a clear indication of the increased role that the government wished schools to have in the selection and training of new entrants to the profession and the second of the documents explicitly stated that the government wanted to *'encourage more universities to follow the example of the integrated working of the best university-school partnerships'* (2011b, p 11). It should be noted that the use of the word 'integrated' is significant and, again, we will return to a discussion of integration within ITE partnerships later in the chapter. Within this new policy context there is little questioning of the premise that more responsibility for schools would necessarily lead to greater integration or to greater quality in a partnership but rather the assumption that this would be the case. And to ensure that partnerships responded in an appropriate way the government indicated that it would

… also change the inspection of ITT so that the quality of partnership working is treated as more important.

(2011b, para 15)

This proposal resulted in a revised framework for the inspection of ITE (Ofsted, 2015), which makes clear that it is the ITE *partnership* that is being inspected, not any single institution within that partnership. Alongside these more recent policy initiatives the government in England commissioned a review of initial teacher training, two of the aims of which were to define effective practice and to recommend where and how improvements could be made (Carter, 2015). The Carter Review, as its report has become known, is premised on the value of effective partnerships, summed up in the assertion in the foreword: *'(t)he truth is that partnership is the key'* (2015, p 3). Its conceptualisation of partnership is, however, clearly influenced by the prevailing policy context; the report goes on to define *'genuine partnerships'* as ones *'where schools play a leading role in the recruitment and selection of trainees, course design and delivery, assessment of trainees and the on-going review of the programmes'* (2015, p 12).

International policy and clinical practice models

Internationally, policy has generally been directed towards providing beginning teachers with more school-based experience, often referred to as '*a practicum turn in teacher education*' (Mattsson et al, 2011, p 17) and with this aim has come an inevitable focus on the nature of the school–university partnership, particularly as a means of addressing perennial issues around the theory–practice divide. In many cases models have been developed that focus on partnership with specific types of schools that are committed not only to the learning of their own pupils but also to full engagement in teacher education (including not only *initial* teacher education but also continuing professional development). In the United States initiatives from the late 1980s onwards, particularly those associated with the Holmes Group (1986), led to the emergence of Professional Development Schools (or 'clinical schools') where innovative teacher education partnerships with publicly funded schools were developed. The intention behind the creation of such schools was to '*connect teacher education reform with school reform*' (Zeichner, 2009, p 26), and they were to '*serve as a setting for clinical internships of pre-service teachers and for in-service professional development of practising teachers*' (Hallinan and Khmelkov, 2001, p 180). Partnership was a key feature of the Professional Development Schools along with an integrated programme within a 'clinical practice' model in which there was strong coherence between the university programme and school (ie 'clinical') experience (Darling-Hammond, 2006a). Likewise clinical practice models, which feature close integration between the different aspects of the teacher education programme through strong university–school partnerships, have been developed in other countries, for example Australia (see McLean Davies et al, 2013 for details), the Netherlands through the introduction of 'academische opleidingsscholen' (Hammerness et al, 2012), and Finland, through designated training schools (Sahlberg, 2012). In seeing teaching as a 'clinical profession', McLean Davies et al emphasise that this

... requires teachers to be able to assess the learning and learning needs of every student and provide appropriate interventions to move that learning forward. Teachers must also have the professional capabilities to evaluate the impact they are having on each student. Moreover, teachers must be expert in gathering evidence and using sound clinical judgement to create appropriate learning strategies to meet each learner's needs. Clinical judgement is only possible if the practice is underpinned by a well-defined body of knowledge, keen observational skills and highly developed analytical skills.

(2013, p 96)

The term 'clinical practice' cannot be used merely to designate the school-based elements of an ITE programme per se, but refers rather to an approach which encapsulates the above extract, reflecting Alter and Coggshall's (2009) summary of the key characteristics of clinical practice professions more widely, which include the '*centrality of the clients*' within it (that is to say, in the case of teaching, the students themselves); a complex professional knowledge base; the use of evidence and judgement (rather than pure technical skill); a community of practice operating with shared standards; and '*rigorous academic and practical training*' (2009, p 9).

For beginning teachers a model of 'clinical practice' preparation

allows them to engage in a process of enquiry: seeking to interpret and make sense of the specific needs of particular students, to formulate and implement particular pedagogical actions and to evaluate the outcomes. While teaching clearly requires mastery of many 'practical' skills, the fundamental importance of 'client' relationships and of 'judgment in action' calls not only for opportunities to rehearse and refine such skills, but also for the chance to engage in the creative processes of interpretation, intervention and evaluation, drawing on diverse sources of knowledge that include research evidence as well as student data.

(Burn and Mutton, 2013, p 3)

Clinical practice models have also emerged elsewhere in the United Kingdom at the institutional level, for example the clinical practice model developed through the Glasgow West Teacher Education Initiative (Conroy et al, 2013) and the Scottish Teachers for a New Era (STNE) programme (Livingston and Shiach, 2010).

Recent developments in Wales, at a national level, have led to the Welsh government's acceptance of the Furlong Report (2015) recommendations, including the need for a *'revised set of accreditation criteria which focus in detail on the nature of university/ school partnerships and which give schools leading responsibilities in key aspects of ITE programmes'* (2015, p 24). Although this appears to echo the *school-led* policy rhetoric that emerged in England from 2010 onwards under the Coalition government, the position in Wales is actually very different. The Furlong Report identified *'little appetite to move away from university led provision'* (2015, p 15) but found that this did not *'necessarily mean that the sector has been well served by contemporary universities'*. The call to give schools greater responsibility within partnerships was a response to the perceived inadequacies of the current system rather than a call for the type of reform that had been seen in England.

Wales has not been alone in commissioning reports into teacher education and those carried out in both Scotland and Northern Ireland (see Donaldson, 2011 and Sahlberg et al, 2014 respectively) have likewise recommended the development of more collaborative approaches to partnership.

Donaldson sees the

need to create a new kind of collaborative partnership within which all aspects of the student's development are a shared responsibility and respective roles and responsibilities are clear.

(2011, p 7)

The authors point out, however, that this sort of collaboration is not easily achieved:

There appears to be no lack of goodwill towards improved partnership working but, although cooperation has improved, effective collaboration remains relatively rare.

(2011, p 48)

The Sahlberg et al (2014) report, when discussing developments in both Scotland and Northern Ireland, points out that while

... in both countries schools have contributed substantially to the professional education of teachers, it is acknowledged that there is still scope for the further strengthening of university/school partnerships, with the aim of securing the closer integration of research and professional practice.

(2014, p 11)

The evolution of practice

The reforms in England that came in the wake of government circular 3/84, and subsequently circulars 9/92 and 14/93, required ITE providers to think in different ways about partnership, with the result that new models began to emerge. There are detailed accounts in the literature of the ways in which some institutions, anticipating these policy trends, acted as pioneers in developing new models of partnership working (see for example, Benton, 1990; Everton and White, 1992; Griffiths and Owen, 1995; McIntyre, 1997; Burton, 1998) but these innovative practices did not necessarily reflect what was happening more widely.

The Modes of Teacher Education (MOTE) project, which was carried out in two phases in order to gain a wider understanding of the impact of these policies on models of teacher education, initially identified three predominant models: *'collaborative partnership'*, *'HEI-led partnership'* and *'separatist partnership'* (Furlong et al, 1996, p 43). It is useful at this point to go back to the researchers' own definitions of these three models.

1. The collaborative model

(A)t the heart of this model is the commitment to develop a training programme where students are exposed to different forms of educational knowledge, some of which come from school, some of which come from HE or elsewhere. Teachers are seen as having an equally legitimate but perhaps different body of professional knowledge from those in higher education. Students are expected and encouraged to use what they learn in school to critique what they learn within the HEI and vice versa. It is through this dialectic that they are expected to build up their own body of professional knowledge. For the model to succeed, teachers and lecturers need opportunities to work and plan together on a regular basis; such on-going collaboration is essential if they are to develop a programme of work for the student that is integrated between the HEI and the school.

(1996, p 44)

2. The higher educational institution (HEI)-led model

(is) led by those in the HEI, though sometimes with the help of a small group of teachers acting as consultants. The aim, as far as course leadership is concerned, is to utilise schools as a resource in setting up learning opportunities for students. Course leaders

have a set of aims which they want to achieve and this demands that schools act in similar ways and make available comparable opportunities for all students. Within this model, quality control – making sure students all receive comparable training opportunities – is a high priority ... The motivation for the HEI-led model may either be pragmatic or principled.

(1996, pp 45–46)

3. The separatist (or complementary) model

The final model of partnership is a separatist one where school and HE are seen as having separate and complementary responsibilities but where there is no systematic attempt to bring these two dimensions into dialogue. In other words there is partnership but not neces-sarily integration in the course; integration is something that the students themselves have to achieve.

(1996, p 47)

The MOTE researchers were keen to point out that '*these models are intended to be seen as ideal typical*' (Furlong et al, 2000, p 77) and went on to say that any '*one individual course might embody aspects of each of these models – either in different parts of the course or for particular groups of students*', setting out what they saw as a '*continuum of possible relationships*'. Overall, however, they found that while a great deal of the rhet-oric around partnership focussed on the collaborative model, the most common of the three in operation at the time was actually the HEI-led model, with programmes almost entirely directed by the HEI, either because this was seen as the most practical way of securing the involvement of schools (which may, at the time, have been reluctant or felt that they did not have the capacity on take on greater levels of responsibility) or because of the commitment of course leaders to a model which was '*antithetical to the demands of partnership*' (Furlong et al, 1996, p 46). Within all three models, however, is the idea of partnership as an '*epistemological and pedagogical concept*' (Furlong et al, 2008), an acknowledgement that beginning teachers need to gain access to different forms of pro-fessional knowledge and that neither the school nor the university alone could provide sufficient learning experiences for effective professional learning to take place (Hagger and McIntyre, 2006). Nevertheless, it is only within a collaborative model in which both the school and the university '*contributes from its own strengths, its own essential purposes, where neither is in the lead, but where each institution learns from the other*' (Furlong, 2013, p 187) that a more fully integrated programme is likely to develop.

The predominance of HEI-led models observed by the MOTE project was undoubtedly challenged by the government reforms of 2010 onwards, which provided a significant stimulus for schools to take on much greater responsibility in all aspects of teacher edu-cation – from the initial selection of candidates to the planning, delivery and evaluation of the programme, including an integral role in the assessment of the beginning teachers. That is not to say that an increase in responsibility has necessarily led to more collabora-tive models – the shift away from HEI-led models may merely have brought about similar complementary (or separatist) models of the sort described by the MOTE researchers (see earlier), without necessarily increasing integration within the programme itself. It is important to recognise the distinction between the leadership of programmes (within school-led models) and the nature of the collaboration within them. Although the Coalition government's policies may have assumed that legislating for the former would inevitably lead to the latter, this may not necessarily have been the case.

There is limited evidence to date about how partnerships have developed as a result of these policy changes, although a report produced by an organisation representing UK universities has noted that the increased involvement of schools has led to more collaboration around programme design and delivery (Universities UK, 2014). Recent research into the impact of the implementation of the School Direct programme in England (Brown et al, 2015) has concluded, however, that there has been a shift in the balance of power within partnership arrangements and that '*(t)he composition of trainee pedagogical experience is being reconfigured*' (2015, p 23) as a result of differing beliefs about the nature of the learning experiences that beginning teachers may need. Their evidence suggests that far from leading to increased collaboration and the development of more integrated programmes, the reforms had led to a situation where

... trainees were having to assimilate quite different understandings of pedagogy between school-based and university-based training sessions whilst efforts to mesh what was being taught within each setting was often limited. It was not uncommon for trainees to feel that content had been repeated by the school and/or university.

(2015, p 23)

This would suggest little more than a version of a complementary partnership in which '*integration is something that the students themselves have to achieve*' (Furlong et al, 1996, p 47).

Teacher education pedagogy within partnership models

When considering partnership as an epistemological and pedagogical concept we are reminded of the first of the two conceptualisations set out by Brisard et al and referred to above, namely the way in which the term is used '*to carry certain theories about the nature of learning to become a teacher*' (2005, p 5). Central to the theories embedded within *partnership* is not just an understanding of what beginning teachers need to know and be able to do, but also of the processes by which such professional learning takes place (Burn et al, 2015). Individual partnership arrangements will take into account a wide range of factors – the way in which school experience is organised and structured, the nature of the support provided by both university and school-based teacher educators, the specific learning tasks that beginning teachers are asked to carry out, the way in which they are expected to make sense of the diverse range of sources from which they can potentially learn etc. – but the extent to which those partnerships are genuinely collaborative will essentially depend on how the various elements of the ITE programme are effectively integrated.

Integration, or programme coherence, defined by Hammerness (2006) as *'the alignment of key ideas and goals across coursework and clinical work'* (p 1244), exerts a powerful influence on the quality of beginning teachers' experience, a point emphasised in two significant recent reports.

First, the British Educational Research Association and the Royal Society for the Encouragement of Arts, Manufactures and Commerce (BERA/RSA) inquiry into research in teacher education (2014), in arguing for the development of what it termed a 'research literate' teaching profession, identified

... the benefits of clinical preparation, through carefully designed programmes of initial teacher education, which allow trainee teachers to integrate knowledge from academic study and research with practical experience in the school and classroom.

(2014, pp 18–19)

Second, the Carter Review (2015) argued that

(p)rogrammes should be structured so there is effective integration between the different types of knowledge and skills trainees need to draw on in order to develop their own teaching. Programmes that privilege either 'theory' or 'practice' fail to take account of the necessity of such integration. What is needed are models of 'clinical practice' (as described by Burn and Mutton (2013)), where trainees have access to the practical wisdom of experts and can engage in a process of enquiry, in an environment where they are able to trial techniques and strategies and evaluate the outcomes.

(2015, p 21)

While 'separatist' (or complementary) and 'HEI-led' models of partnership may result in effective coverage of the required elements of a programme across different settings, coverage which can be clearly audited, it is only a fully collaborative model that can come close to ensuring that there is the necessary integration of these different elements. Many researchers have identified that such integration can best be achieved only through approaches which focus on 'clinical practice', referred to in both reports cited earlier, and that it is only through such an approach that we can start to eradicate the unhelpful *'conceptual binary around "theory/ practice"'* and a related *'universities / schools' divide'* (Murray and Mutton, 2015, p 70).

But how do programmes that adopt these approaches operate? As mentioned earlier, programmes that incorporate clinical practice approaches have been adopted by institutions in many countries, including the emergence of Professional Development Schools in the United States (see Teitel, 1988, for a review of early work around this development) and the Teachers for a New Era initiative (Carnegie Corporation, 2001). In examining teacher education programmes that were based on close cooperation with the Professional Development Schools, Darling-Hammond (2006b) identifies the three key *'critical components'* of effective provision as being

tight coherence and integration among courses and between course work and clinical work in schools, extensive and intensely supervised clinical work integrated with course work using pedagogies that link theory and practice, and closer, proactive relationships with schools that serve diverse learners effectively and develop and model good teaching.

(Darling-Hammond, 2006b, p 300)

The two-year Masters in Teaching at the University of Melbourne is another such programme that places significant emphasis on collaborative partnership working as an integral part of the clinical preparation of teachers where

(u)nderpinning the programme delivery is the principle that universities and schools must work in close partnership if this vision of clinical teaching is to be modelled in pre-service teacher education.

(Mclean Davies et al, 2003, p 96)

In England, one of the few collaborative partnership models identified by the MOTE researchers (Furlong et al, 1996) was the Oxford Internship Scheme (Benton, 1990), developed and implemented before circulars 9/92 and 14/93 had been published but signalling a more radical approach to teacher education than had been considered elsewhere at the time. Drawing on research evidence the programme rejected the traditional 'theory-into-practice' model (one which had assumed that it would be relatively unproblematic to ask beginning teachers to apply decontextualised knowledge, acquired at the university, in very diverse school contexts) and based the new programme on a set of clearly defined principles, including strong notions of partnership expressed in the following ways: joint planning of the ITE programme; clear and explicit relationships and short time intervals between the different elements; carefully graduated learning tasks; explicit encouragement for the beginning teachers to use ideas from diverse sources; and an emphasis on testing all ideas against the different criteria valued in each context (McIntyre, 1990, p 32–33). Above all was the need for effective integration of all aspects of the programme, and in particular the distinctive contributions of both the school and the university within a collaborative partnership model.

Within such models the organisation and structure of the partnership do not become an end in themselves, but rather the means by which the learning model of the programme can be delivered in order to '*achieve a common goal – that of educating professional teachers with the knowledge, skills and dispositions necessary to more effectively teach diverse students*' (Tatto, 1996, p 176). There is, however, the danger that in adopting simplistic notions of what partnership entails this common goal can become somewhat lost and result in an increased focus on procedural matters. Furlong et al (2006), reporting on the findings of their evaluation of the National Partnership Project (NPP) in England, identified the way in which increased collaboration between ITE providers and schools (as well as with other providers), while having some benefits at local level, often resulted in the emphasis shifting away from the '*complex task of bringing together partners who provide access to different conceptions of professional knowledge*' (2006, p 41). Furthermore

... when partnership is reduced to 'finding more places' or setting up common procedures and paper work, without paying attention to the epistemological and pedagogical issues

underpinning any one particular teacher education programme, it undermines the nature of the professional education that is offered. Once again, it flattens complexity and reduces teacher education to technical rationalist tasks.

(2006, p 41)

One of the initiatives developed within the NPP was the establishment of Training Schools, that is to say schools which received this designation from the government following previous strong involvement in teacher education partnership work. Their role was to develop and share good practice both in and beyond their own immediate networks and they received specific funding to facilitate this work. With the demise of the NPP in 2005 these schools were able to retain their designation but received no further funding, although many subsequently became Teaching Schools under a new initiative set up by the Coalition government in 2011 (see DfE, 2014 for full details). Although these schools have been funded to take a leading role in ITE, continuing professional development and school-to-school support they are not conceptualised in the same way as some of the international 'training school' models described earlier (eg the 'academische opleidingsscholen' in the Netherlands and the 'Harjoittelukoulut' – teacher training schools – in Finland). Nevertheless the Coalition government did want to promote university–school partnership models along the lines of these international models (particularly the Finnish training school model) and proposed the establishment of

... a few innovative and prestigious University Training Schools (UTSs) in England. These will be aligned with the essential elements of training schools in Finland. These go significantly beyond the traditional partnership arrangements that some universities currently have with schools. UTSs will be run by some of our best providers of ITT and will deliver three core functions: teaching children, training teachers and undertaking research. Universities will be responsible for running UTSs and will operate outside the maintained sector as academies/free schools, so that a governance model can be put in place to give the university the appropriate level of control.

(DfE, 2011b, p 13)

The proposals, however, focussed primarily on the governance of such schools rather than on the nature of any training programme of which they were to be an integral part (the 'essential elements' referred to in the DfE policy document). To date in England there are currently only two such schools in operation (the University of Cambridge Primary School and the University of Birmingham School), both of which promote the strong links with their respective university and with its teacher education programmes, as well as the role that research plays in the school. These schools are very much in the first stages of their development so it remains to be seen to what extent, if at all, they come to exemplify the 'essential elements' of the Finnish teacher training schools.

IN A **NUTSHELL**

Effective teacher education partnerships are essential in ensuring the supply of sufficient numbers of high-quality teachers for our schools. For many years government policy has recognised the importance of partnership working but the rhetoric around partnership had not always been matched by actual practice, leading to the view among some that too much control lay in the hands of HEI providers. The 'school-led' policy drive has attempted to re-align this balance of power by setting up structures intended to give schools more responsibility for the recruitment and training of new teachers, but changes to structure and organisation do not necessarily mean that underlying pedagogic approaches also change significantly. The key question is not just where specific content is delivered and by whom, but rather *how* the learning experiences of beginning teachers are planned collaboratively and delivered in an integrated way.

REFLECTIONS ON **CRITICAL ISSUES**

Partnership has long been at the heart of ITE programmes but the nature of partnership working has changed significantly as schools have (generally as a result of specific government policy) assumed an increasing role in the training of new teachers. The acceptance of partnership as something good in its own right, and of the accompanying rhetoric around partnership working, can mask more fundamental issues of concern related to the ways in which teacher education pedagogy is enacted across diverse settings. Where partnerships are more fully collaborative in nature then such issues may be less pronounced, but where each partner has designated, but separate, responsibilities the degree of integration and coherence across the programme is likely to be reduced.

CRITICAL **ISSUES**

- *What are the issues that challenge the ability of ITE partnerships to work effectively?*
- *How might some of these issues be addressed?*

The intractable issues

Returning to Alexander's conclusion that *'the comfortable language of "partnership" conceals more intractable issues'* (1984, p 142), it is worth considering what some of these issues might be in relation to current conceptualisations of partnership working. Conroy et al (2013) also warn of the dangers inherent in the *'comfortable language of partnership'* and argue that

[t]he rhetorical power of 'partnership' is deeply embedded in contemporary forms of governance. It works to conceal differences in political and academic representations of the purpose and value of work-based learning for prospective teachers.

(2013, p 558)

So how do such differences manifest themselves?

1. Partners may not necessarily share the same conceptualisation of what constitutes effective teacher preparation

Differing conceptualisations may relate to either the knowledge base that beginning teachers need, or the process of professional learning by which they acquire the necessary knowledge, skills and understanding to enable them to teach effectively, or perhaps both. In England, teacher education policy at national level from 2010 onwards privileged the view that

(t)eaching is a craft and it is best learnt as an apprentice observing a master craftsman or woman. Watching others, and being rigorously observed yourself as you develop, is the best route to acquiring mastery in the classroom.

(Gove, 2010)

The development of the School Direct model was based on this premise and led to the emergence of many new partnership models that challenged the traditional approaches of what the MOTE researchers (Furlong et al, 2000) had described as 'HEI-led' models, in which key decisions had often been taken by the ITE provider – often a university. This new approach encouraged schools to take an equal, if not leading, role in partnership working, but this may not necessarily have led to agreement between the partners as to the most effective method of preparing new teachers for the profession, nor necessarily to more innovative ways of working within partnerships. Brown et al, in their study of the School Direct initiative, highlight the way in which

(i)ncreasingly, teaching is conceived in craft-based, technicist terms strengthened by increasing prescription and performativity measures, which require teachers to present and shape knowledge in particular ways. Within this context, conceptions of the relationship between theory and practice have been progressively replaced by conceptions of practice that integrate situated conceptions of theory responsive to the needs of practice. Furthermore, many re-conceptualisations of teacher education have privileged practical components to the detriment of theory and analysis.

(Brown et al, 2015, p 5)

Although the critique clearly arises from one specific policy, differences in the way in which separate partners view what constitutes the effective preparation of teachers can also co-exist within more traditional programmes, often reflecting the *'disconnect between the campus and school-based components of programs'* (Zeichner, 2010, p 89). This is not just about the structure of programmes but also about the underlying beliefs of those engaged in teacher education programmes in whatever capacity. For partnerships to work effectively there needs to be *'a common, clear vision of good teaching that permeates all coursework and clinical experiences, creating a coherent set of learning experiences'* (Darling-Hammond, 2014, p 548), but this is not always the case. Bartholomew and Sandholtz (2009) argue that even where there may be initial agreement as to the goals of a teacher education programme, these can diverge over time and compromise what the partnership is trying to achieve. Furthermore *'differing perspectives about the role of the teacher'* (2009, p 164) can have an effect on the realisation of these programme goals. Their study found a tension between school officials who wanted to produce teachers who would be able to *'deliver an established curriculum'* and university partners who were more interested in promoting *'teacher expertise and decision making'* (2009, p 164). Taylor (2008, p 65) alerts us to the danger that *'any conflicting expectations and beliefs will result in student learning being fragmented – between theory and practice, thought and action – rather than seamless'*.

Zeichner believes that these discontinuities can only be addressed within truly collaborative programmes where there is mutual respect between partners for the distinctive contribution that each can make and where there are agreed approaches to beginning teachers' learning:

These efforts involve a shift in the epistemology of teacher education from a situation where academic knowledge is seen as the authoritative source of knowledge about teaching to one where different aspects of expertise that exist in schools and communities are brought into teacher education and coexist on a more equal plane with academic knowledge. This broader view about the kinds of expertise that are needed to educate teachers expands opportunities for teacher learning, as new synergies are created through the interplay of knowledge from different sources.

(Zeichner, 2010, p 95)

2. There may be tensions between the differing goals of preparing a teacher to be *school ready* or *profession-ready*

The School Direct policy initiative has provided schools with the opportunity both to recruit (directly and at a local level) the teachers these schools have identified as being able to fill school vacancies, and to train them. The notion of 'growing your own' has been popular and has allowed schools to continue to work with ITE providers while at the same time having greater autonomy in determining the nature of the training programme. This can, however, lead to tensions. Given the *'culture of competitive performativity'* that Ball (2003, p 219) describes and which pervades the professional contexts in which beginning teachers will eventually be working, there is a need not just to develop teachers who are equipped to work in one context. The potential tensions here are clear – if a school regards the purpose of the training programme as essentially to prepare teachers to work in the specific context of that school then it is likely that the focus will be on the enculturation of those teachers into the specific practices and ways of working in that one particular setting. What may be of a lesser priority, perhaps, is the development of the beginning teachers' capacity to be responsive and innovative in the face of contexts which will inevitably change, often as a result of local or national policy trends. While all beginning teachers are required to reach a level of practical competence in the classroom so that they can perform particular tasks efficiently and effectively, they also have to be able to innovate, that is to say to *'move beyond existing routines... to rethink key ideas, practices'* (Hammerness et al, 2005, pp 358–359). Furthermore, they also have to be able to continue to learn while these contexts are changing and this requires the *'capacity for critical engagement with suggested innovations in classroom practice'* (Hagger and McIntyre, 2006, p 37).

Partnerships need to work in a way that affords beginning teachers the learning opportunities which support them in developing their capacity for innovative practice by equipping them with the appropriate criteria (both academic and practical) by which to evaluate such innovation. Where the scope for this development is limited there is the danger that the focus reverts to an expectation that it is sufficient for the beginning teacher to deliver the required curriculum in an agreed manner, what Edwards and Protheroe (2004) refer to as *'teaching by proxy'* (2004, p 183). This inevitably leads to a tendency for more prescription (following existing tried and tested approaches), less innovative practice and little opportunity to evaluate the success or otherwise of the approach taken in light of the evidence of alternative approaches. McIntyre (2009) also alerts us to this danger and argues that partnership models are often *'aimed only at preparing beginning teachers for the status quo, and very deliberately being planned to avoid them being encouraged to think critically of that status quo'* (2009, p 603).

3.   Partners have differing priorities and differing levels of accountability

It has been noted in many of the commentaries that accompanied the policy developments in England from the 1980s onwards that while HEI providers are required to establish formal partnerships with schools there is no parallel requirement for schools to engage in initial teacher education. For the majority that do, however, it is never the primary focus of the school's activity – which always remains the education of its own pupils. Notwithstanding the perceived advantages (such as the exposure to innovative pedagogy, the wider professional development benefits of involvement with mentoring and the development of a *'culture of discourse'* around professional learning (Mutton and Butcher, 2008) a school's ITE involvement can be demanding and has the potential to be seen as something that detracts from, rather than enhances, pupil learning.

While schools are responsible for the performance of their pupils accredited ITE providers are accountable for the quality of the teacher education programme and the effective working of the partnership. In addition to the need to demonstrate compliance with a range of statutory requirements, partnerships must also demonstrate that they prepare their beginning teachers sufficiently well to enable them to meet the requirements of the appropriate professional standards.

Finally, resourcing is a related issue since teacher education partnerships tend to rely on goodwill from schools and the limited funding available to schools may not necessarily cover *real* costs. New partnership models (especially those associated with the development of School Direct) can be *'extremely resource-intensive in terms of administration for both universities and schools'* (McNamara and Murray, 2013, p 16) putting further pressure on considerations of a fair distribution of labour between partners with the limited resources available leading to the potential *'underresourcing of clinical experiences'* (Zeichner and Bier, 2014, p 107). This is perhaps most obviously reflected in the amount of time and resources that can reasonably be devoted to mentoring beginning teachers, given the other responsibilities that teachers have and the responsibilities to their own pupils. The overall lack of consistency in the quality of mentoring across partnerships is by no means an issue unique to England and is well documented in the international literature, but the complex nature of partnership arrangements in this country may exacerbate the issues rather than reduce them.

4.   Schools often engage in complex partnership arrangements with different ITE providers

For many years schools have become used to working in partnership with a range of different providers, although many smaller schools (particularly in the primary sector) may still work predominantly with one provider within a fairly traditional model. Where there is diverse provision – either across subjects in a secondary school, with different providers offering different subjects, or offering School Direct (perhaps both salaried and fee-paying programmes) alongside more traditional programmes in the same subject area – there are likely to be *'complex relationships at work within multiple partnerships'* (Mutton and Butcher, 2008, p 60). This may involve differences across a number of areas relating to, for example, course structure, variable patterns of time in school, programme documentation, assessment processes, mentoring requirements and the nature and frequency of school-based training elements. Within such a context the temptation may understandably be to rationalise where possible in order to achieve coherence across the trainees' experiences in the school, but Furlong et al (2006) warn that such approaches can lead to a position where

(t)he complexity and contestability of professional knowledge is therefore no longer seen to be at the heart of what partnership is about; professional knowledge becomes simplified, flattened, it is essentially about contemporary practice in schools.

(Furlong et al, 2006, p 41)

5. The quality of mentoring across all partnerships is variable

One of the key *'intractable issues'* faced by programmes of teacher education, both in this country and internationally, is the variability in the quality of support provided to beginning teachers, often related to the quality of school-based mentoring (Hobson et al, 2009). Jones and Straker (2006) concluded from their study of over one hundred mentors involved in both 'traditional' and 'employment-based' routes associated with one higher education provider that

mentors draw primarily on their professional practice and personal experience acquired as teachers, and that in their work with trainees and newly qualified teachers they tend to replicate strategies they use with their pupils. In fulfilling their role as mentors effectively they appear to focus primarily on the repertoire of teacher behaviour prescribed by 'the standards' as well as their school's goals, perhaps at the expense of other equally important aspects of professional training and development, such as making sense of wider educational issues.

(2006, pp 181–182)

This was recognised as an issue in the Carter Review (2015) and its recommendations led to the publication of national standards for school-based mentors (DfE, 2016a) as a mechanism for securing more consistency in terms of the support that beginning teachers receive. It could be argued, however, that these approximate more to what McIntyre and Hagger (1993) referred to as *'minimal mentoring'* (p 95), that is to say mentoring that involves a designated mentor coordinating and supervising the beginning teacher's school-based experiences, particularly in terms of the planning and delivery of lessons. These national standards require mentors to demonstrate that, in addition to having specific personal qualities, they are able to '*(s)upport trainees to develop their teaching practice in order to set high expectations of all pupils and to meet their needs*' (DfE, 2016a, p 11) and '*set high expectations and induct the trainee to understand their role and responsibilities as a teacher*' (p 12) but do not address the nature of how mentors can support beginning teachers' professional learning more effectively.

Addressing the issues

Notwithstanding the potential difficulties inherent in partnership working there can nevertheless be ways in which partnerships are able to operate successfully. The Carter Review (2015) highlighted what it judged to be three key features of effective partnership, namely the use of expertise from across the partnership; mutual respect and a shared vision, as well as clearly defined and agreed roles; and a critical mass of expertise achieved through diversity within the partnership which should include the opportunity for beginning teachers to learn from a range of different settings (2015, p 42). While acknowledging that these are important issues they nevertheless concern the ideal *conditions* of partnership rather than the *quality* of the professional learning that might result from partnerships operating within such conditions. So what might influence the quality and coherence of the professional learning programme?

First there needs to be agreement as to the type of teacher that the programme is designed to produce. There is likely to be little coherence if insufficient discussion has taken place as to the knowledge, skills and understanding which those undertaking the programme are expected to acquire. Without such discussion there are likely to be unexplored assumptions on both sides, informed by particular institutional histories or practices or in many cases by the personal experiences of training of those working within the partnership. Just as beginning teachers will have specific pre-conceptions as to what it means to be a good teacher and how this expertise might be acquired (Pendry, 1997; Hagger and McIntyre, 2006) it is likely that teacher educators will also have such pre-conceptions which will, in turn, strongly influence the way in which they conceive of the aims of any training programme. Exploring these beliefs can be fruitful, lead to a better understanding of the perspectives of all those involved in the partnership and help secure agreed aims for the programme.

Second, having secured such agreement, there can be further discussion as to the content of the programme and the way in which it might then be structured and delivered in order to enable these programme aims to be met. Again, this will need to be informed by appropriate institutional histories and practices and take into account commonly agreed understandings of what needs to be taught, when it will be taught and by whom.

Third, in considering the delivery of the ITE programme, the partners can agree on what expertise is available and how such expertise will be drawn effectively so that beginning teachers can maximise the learning potential from the different contexts available to them.

From the school's perspective, given that teacher education is likely to be one of many additional competing concerns, this cannot be left to chance or depend on the willingness or capacity of individual school-based mentors to engage with the programme, or to engage in 'minimal mentoring' (McIntyre and Hagger 1993, p 95). Effective partnerships will work strategically to minimise the risk of variability in the quality of mentoring through agreed approaches to beginning teachers' learning, effective mentor training that focuses on pedagogical as well as organisational issues, collaborative decision making and a regular review of programme provision.

Finally, those responsible for planning and delivering a teacher education programme need to acknowledge that the 'intractable issues' cannot be ignored. Nor can they be dealt with by placing undue emphasis on immediate organisational arrangements at the expense of teacher education pedagogy. All those involved in the partnership should be in a position to be able to address the issues critically and to seek collaborative ways forward as any partnership continues to evolve.

IN A **NUTSHELL**

ITE partnerships are inherently complex and in order for them to work successfully they have to engage with a number of challenging issues. They require institutions with quite different histories, cultures and practices to come together for a particular purpose (the training of potential new entrants to the profession through the delivery of an agreed ITE programme); in many cases this is a primary activity for one of the partners while for the other it is a secondary, and perhaps even peripheral, activity. What it is that these beginning teachers need to know, and to be able to do, as well as the process by which such knowledge and skills are developed, is not easily agreed upon. Where shared understandings do not exist there may inevitably be tensions, both in relation to the organisational aspects of partnership working as well as to pedagogical concerns. Successful approaches to ITE partnerships are, however, possible but require constant scrutiny through the ongoing evaluation of the programme and its day-to-day practices.

REFLECTIONS ON **CRITICAL ISSUES**

Different priorities and objective motives are likely to be factors that challenge the potential for effective partnership working, giving rise to possible tensions at both a conceptual level and at the level of practice. It may be that these issues are not 'intractable', as Alexander (1984) suggested, but neither should they be ignored or concealed by the rhetoric around partnership. If tensions are recognised and explored as collaborative working develops then it is likely that partnerships can mature within a context of mutual understanding and respect. If, however, partnership is viewed predominantly in terms of its structural and organisational aspects (for example, in relation to the way in which the programme is delivered in both settings, the nature of the assessment of the beginning teachers and the way in which the provision is quality assured), then the 'flattening' to which Furlong et al (2006) refer is more likely to occur.

CRITICAL **ISSUES**

- *How is partnership being enacted within the new policy context?*
- *How is the ITE curriculum being conceptualised within school-led models of teacher education?*
- *How are specific roles within new models of partnership being defined?*

Introduction

Our answers to the questions outlined earlier draw on a case study of the way in which one recently accredited SCITT provider is developing its understanding of what partnership working entails. The chapter will demonstrate the complexity of the context (which is not atypical) and present a picture of the way in which the ITE programme itself is being conceptualised, as well as the nature of the roles and responsibilities within it. We have selected this particular school for the case study because it has always been interested in new developments in teacher education and has fully and enthusiastically embraced the recent policy agenda. Following the presentation of the case study, we draw on it in subsequent chapters to illustrate the evolving nature of partnership within the new policy context.

Data for the case study were drawn from individual semi-structured interviews (each lasting approximately 35 minutes) with 15 key personnel involved in ITE within the school. Interview participants were asked about

- » their own background and professional experience;
- » their views about what constitute the core features of an effective ITE programme;
- » what facilitates and potentially constrains their teacher education role within the school;
- » how they see the particular programme with which they are involved;
- » their role within the planning and evaluation of the ITE curriculum;
- » the perceived advantages and disadvantages of working either within either a single ITE programme or with other providers;
- » and any potential recommendations they might have for changes to the programme in question.

Prior to the interview the interviewees completed a short questionnaire outlining their roles and responsibilities, their overall time in the role to date, any relevant prior experience, specific training for the role, the time officially allocated to their particular area of respon-sibility and the time judged to be spent each week carrying out the role. All data collection was subject to appropriate ethical approval. Pseudonyms have been used throughout.

Case study: Waterside Academy

Background

Waterside Academy is not new to involvement in teacher education partnership working. Even before the requirements of Circular 9/92 led to the greater participation of schools in ITE programmes the school was a key partner within the Oxford Internship Scheme (see Benton, 1990 for details). The scheme, which was developed in the mid-1980s and, as mentioned in Chapter 1, identified by the MOTE researchers as one of the few genu-inely collaborative partnership models in existence in England at the time (Furlong et al, 1996), involved school partners in the planning, delivery and evaluation of the complete ITE programme. The university PGCE programme trains approximately 190 new teachers each year and Waterside has, since the inception of the scheme, maintained a record of unbroken partnership with the university and has consistently offered placements across a range of curriculum subject areas. In addition, it had, until recently, also been involved in partnership working with a number of other ITE providers in order to ensure a sufficient range of subject coverage within the school.

To give some broader context, Waterside is an 11–19 secondary school of just over 1700 pupils with the following features.

> » It is a high-performing school, judged to be 'outstanding' by Ofsted.

> » It consistently performs above the average (for schools both locally and nation-ally) in terms of examination results.

> » The school has a significant number of pupils from above-average socio-economic backgrounds but also a significant number from less advantaged backgrounds.

> » Eligibility for free school meals is in line with the national average.

> » The proportion of pupils from minority ethnic backgrounds is higher than the national average.

> » The percentage of pupils with English as an additional language is higher than the national average.

> » While the school population reflects the national average in terms of the percentage of pupils with learning difficulties and/or disabilities (LDD), it includes a higher than average proportion of pupils with statements of special educational need (SEN).

The school has responded positively to a range of policy reforms first set out in the Coalition government's 2010 White Paper, 'The Importance of Teaching' (DfE, 2010). It became a 'converter academy' in 2012 (that is to say, it chose academy status in order to benefit from greater levels of autonomy allowed by the Coalition government's policy reforms in 2010

(DfE, 2016b)). In 2013 Waterside became the lead school within a Multi-Academy Trust, which has grown to include six primary schools and three further secondary schools in the local area, and a new Free School governed by the trust is due to open in the near future.

The school received teaching school status in 2013 (see DfE, 2014 for details of teaching school requirements) and was designated as a SCITT provider in 2014, offering both salaried and tuition-fee School Direct (SD) programmes for just over 80 trainees in both primary and secondary school subjects. Nationally, SD (salaried) trainees are graduates who usually have three or more years' work experience and are employed as an unqualified teacher by the school in which they are training. The government provides funding to cover training costs and to subsidise the trainee salaries. SD tuition-fee places are open to all graduates and are funded by fees paid by the trainee who may be eligible for a training bursary. In both cases the school works in partnership with an accredited ITE provider, which can be either a university or a SCITT. At Waterside many of the staff have previously been involved as mentors within other ITE partnership programmes and now have designated roles within the SCITT. It should be noted that alongside its work as an accredited ITE provider in its own right, the school remains a member of the long-standing partnership programme with the local university, accepting a number of its student teachers each year.

Teacher education at Waterside Academy

As the lead school in the SCITT, Waterside has a number of staff with responsibility for ITE, including an overall SCITT director, who is responsible for the day-to-day management of the training programmes offered (currently, the SD salaried programme and the SD tuition-fee, or 'non-salaried' programme as it is referred to within the SCITT). The director liaises with schools within the partnership (currently 59 primary schools and 30 secondary schools) and, in conjunction with the SCITT Board of Governors, is responsible for the strategic direction of the scheme. The director is supported by two programme leaders (one each for the salaried and non-salaried programmes respectively). Within the school each associate teacher (as the trainees are called) is assigned a subject-specific mentor who works with the associate teacher on a day-to-day basis within the subject area in question. There is also a designated 'subject lead specialist', responsible for each subject across the wider SCITT and many of them are also based at Waterside. These specialists also act as 'visiting tutors' for the subject in question, which entails carrying out monitoring visits to other schools within the partnership where associate teachers have been placed. In addition there is a 'senior link' teacher with quality assurance responsibilities across the partnership and two 'well-being coaches' employed centrally by the SCITT. The work of the SCITT is further supported by a part-time compliance officer (a former teacher at the school), a SCITT manager and a programme administrator.

Interviews were carried out with the following people: all those based at the school with a managerial role within the SCITT; a representative sample of subject-specific mentors (four in total); and three members of staff involved with the established university PGCE partnership – two subject mentors and the professional tutor (who co-ordinates the overall training programme of the student teachers in the school). An overview of those involved in the data collection is summarised in Table 3.1.

Table 3.1 Overview of those included in the case study

Name	Role	Time assigned to the role	Time in the role to date	Experience prior to taking on the role (as identified by respondents)
Paul	SCITT director	85% of his role as Assistant Headteacher	3 years	20 years teaching experience. Member of the school's senior leadership team. Previous experience of being a mentor.
Terry	SD salaried leader	0.7 fte	3 years	Previous mentoring experience within the local HEI partnership. Part-time secondment (1 day per week for 2 years) to work as a subject tutor on the university PGCE programme.
Lisa	SD tuition-fee leader	0.7 fte	5 months	Background in teaching and special needs education. Previous role within the SCITT.
Kerry	SD senior link	0.2 fte	2 years	Previous mentoring experience within the local HEI partnership; worked as the school's professional tutor within the PGCE programme. CPD responsibilities within the school. Counselling qualification. Middle leadership training.
Beth	Joint subject lead specialist	Depends on time of year.	2 years	9 years teaching experience in United Kingdom and the United States. Masters level qualification (from the United States).
Nigel	Joint subject lead specialist	2 hours per week	2 years	Teaching experience.

(continued)

Table 3.1 (Cont.)

Name	Role	Time assigned to the role	Time in the role to date	Experience prior to taking on the role (as identified by respondents)
Faith	Subject specialist	2 hours per week	1 year	Previous mentoring experience within the local HEI partnership.
Dominic	Subject specialist	2 hours per week.	1 year	Previous mentoring experience within the local HEI partnership.
Val	SD mentor	1 hour (allocated mentor time).	2 years	No prior experience.
Poppy	SD mentor	1 hour (allocated mentor time).	2 years	No prior experience.
Caroline	SD mentor	1 hour (allocated mentor time).	1 year	Previous mentoring experience within the local HEI partnership.
Beatrice	SD mentor	1 hour	1 year	No prior experience.
James	PGCE mentor	1 hour every 2 weeks (allocated mentor time).	3 years	Mentor training, middle leadership training; training for coaching.
Simon	PGCE mentor	1 hour every 2 weeks (allocated mentor time).	13 years	Mentor training over a number of years within two local HEI partnerships.
Sonia	PGCE professional tutor	4 hours per week	2 years	Previous experience as a mentor within the local HEI partnership, and mentoring experience within one other partnership.

What do Waterside teacher educators see as the core components of an effective training programme?

The SCITT director and the two programme leaders (salaried and non-salaried) articulate a range of factors which they believe constitute the core features of an effective teacher education programme. They cite the need for such a programme to prepare trainees to become competent classroom practitioners and fully capable of taking on the challenges they will face the following year as a newly qualified teacher (NQT). Central to this is the need for 'significant and substantial school placements' and effective systems of support, including the provision of high-quality mentoring, all framed within a programme that enables the trainees to see beyond the immediate context in which they are working. This is expressed as the need to be 'challenged in terms of their reflections in different contexts' or be equipped sufficiently well to be able to question what lies behind 'the debates and issues within their subjects'. Similar views about the value of seeing beyond a single context are expressed by the mentors within the SCITT programme who also talk about needing to have a 'streamlined structure' and 'good placement schools', the need for training that effectively prepares the trainee teachers for their future role, as well as the importance of strong mentoring. One of the School Direct mentors, along with the SD (salaried) programme leader, highlights the importance of subject-specific support rather than purely a generic approach. Unsurprisingly, perhaps, the senior link teacher also emphasises the need for both 'supportive but also challenging quality assurance' and 'academic rigour'. The four subject specialists, who also act as visiting tutors for the SCITT, reiterate many of the points mentioned. One talks about 'the need for "a combination of theory and practice"' and another talks about about 'having the pedagogical input put in, in a school setting' so that 'teachers and trainers as well can figure out what works and what doesn't work'. Both see the subject-specific contribution as essential. A third specialist argues for a programme that 'genuinely prepares trainees for life in the classroom' and the fourth believes that any programme should be flexible enough to be able to respond to the individual needs of each of the associate teachers.

Overall the teachers involved in the SCITT programme are consistent in their views – not all mention the same features of an effective programme but all generally agree that a classroom-focussed training programme with a clear structure and appropriate levels of support throughout (including strong mentoring) are essential elements of any such programme.

The perspectives of the two mentors working within the university-linked PGCE programme are broadly similar. Both discuss the relationship between theory and practice but while the one is clear that practical experience in the classroom should *precede* any theoretical input, the other argues more strongly for greater integration of the two elements and that 'teaching needs to be studied as well as practised'. He says that he has some concerns that the School Direct approach minimises the theoretical component and 'mistakes teaching for being something that you can do with an apprenticeship'. Sonia, the professional tutor for the PGCE programme, emphasises the need to provide trainee teachers with the tools to enable them to reflect effectively on their own practice and considers that observation is an essential part of that process – both the trainee's observation of experienced teachers and observation of the trainee's own teaching.

The school's role in the planning of the ITE curriculum

There is consensus among those involved in the SCITT programme that the planning of the ITE curriculum is primarily carried out by the SCITT director and the two SD programme leaders. The director sees the process as being one based on feedback from a wide range of stakeholders ('*we consult very widely – previous trainees, current trainees, mentors, senior links in schools, head teachers*') and one that is carried out with an awareness of wider statutory and accountability guidelines, such as government requirements and the Ofsted inspection framework. The individual programme leaders reinforce the idea of the programme being responsive to evaluative feedback and the analysis of programme data related to trainee progression throughout the course of the training period. There is reference to the wider governance of the SCITT and it is clear that both the governing body and the separate steering group are key to the strategic direction of the SCITT and to decisions regarding overall programme content, although it is the steering group that has most influence over '*the appropriateness of the content and the method of delivery*'. The director also emphasises the efforts that are made to integrate the focus of the centrally delivered content with what is occurring in the actual school placements. Once the overall programme content has been agreed, the two programme leaders then '*shape that into the calendar*'. Many of the SCITT mentors refer to the '*spine*', which is the way in which the overall programme structure is understood. One of the subject lead specialists describes the spine as the way in which '*the central training sessions form a more generic basis*' and the way in which the subject specialists will then '*tailor*' the content of the spine '*to the specific needs of their subject*'. He notes, however, that the primary trainees within the SCITT programme generally receive less subject-specific input as the primary specialist will not have a subject-specific role and will therefore tend to deliver more generic sessions within the overall primary programme.

The mentors' view is that programme directors are responsible for planning the programme, the details of which are all in the handbook. The mentors then deal with issues that they have been asked to cover, adapting their input as appropriate to suit the subject-specific context, although a review of the subject content has been carried out with a view '*to make it more streamlined*'. The handbook is a central document within the SCITT and contains a summary of all the school-based tasks (a recent innovation), the aim of the latter being to integrate more fully the central 'spine' with the individual subject-specific content. Most mentors state that they have little or no role in the process of planning, either of the central spine or of the subject-specific content (which is usually carried out by the subject lead specialists). One SCITT mentor says, however, that she plans the subject-specific element in collaboration with her head of department, who is the subject lead specialist, and that this enables her to tailor the content to meet the needs of the individual trainee at any given time in the training year. The mentors emphasise that the planning is not 'set in stone' and that there is welcome flexibility if one aspect of the programme or another is not seen to be working well, or is judged not to be at the right time within the overall training programme. The subject specialists themselves plan the content of the individual subject pedagogy sessions, guided by the framework of the 'spine', which gives an indication of the broad topic areas to be covered at any given time, although with some flexibility for adaptation as appropriate. Overall there is an acknowledgement that the core structure of the programme is planned by the director, in conjunction with the individual programme leaders, but that this 'lofty level of decision making' (as one of the lead specialists characterises it) is very responsive to feedback as the programme evolves.

One of the two mentors working with the PGCE programme sees that the planning of the programme is also not something in which he has any direct involvement since this is the responsibility of the Partnership Committee (the steering group for the PGCE pro-gramme). Here planning is carried out 'at a very high level', with the PGCE course director responsible for its implementation. The mentor sees his role as primarily putting together a timetable for the student teacher and in responding to any development targets that have been set through the process of observation and feedback. The other subject mentor did, however, talk about the collaborative aspects of the planning involving the university and the group of subject mentors and the way in which feedback from both mentors and trainees leads to adaptations of the programme as time went on. The professional tutor also cites the university as being the driver of the overall planning of the PGCE course but sees her role as planning an appropriate school-based professional studies programme (which includes a weekly session for all the PGCE student teachers in the school), which complements the university-based programme.

The evaluation of the ITE programme

Likewise, much of the responsibility for evaluating both programmes offered by the SCITT rests with the director and the programme leaders. In addition to informal feedback and monitoring of the taught sessions (all the subject specialists comment on having been observed at some point by the SCITT director and/or the programme lead tutors during their subject-specific training sessions) there is an extensive formal evaluation cycle. This comprises a mid-year review and end-of-year evaluation, both of which involve online questionnaires to elicit feedback from trainees, mentors, subject specialists and visiting tutors, senior links within each of the partnership schools and previous trainees now working as NQTs. This process is supported by focus group interviews that represent the views of relevant stakeholders; the programme also has an external moderator. Finally, the recent appointment of a quality assurance officer, based within the school, provides a further layer of accountability measures within the SCITT. Individual mentors emphasise the way in which informal feedback from the trainees helps determine the direction that any individual support might take.

Since many of the visiting subject tutors within the SCITT are based at the school, a visiting tutor from another school will usually be required to make visits to Waterside in order to provide some external moderation. These colleagues from other local schools are seen as providing another level of quality assurance across the partnership as a whole. One mentor gives the example of a visiting tutor's recommendations that her own trainee's timetable be reduced to bring it into line with that of other trainees across the partnership and thereby provide the associate teacher in question with more time for reflection. Another mentor also highlights the important role that these colleagues play:

They're coming, they're reading all the paperwork ... they're meeting with the associate teacher, they're meeting with us to see if the progress of the associate teacher is suitable. Is the programme and what the school is doing, is it benefitting the associate teacher?

It is recognised that the specific ITE practice in operation at Waterside may not necessarily reflect practice that is consistent across the SCITT partnership as a whole; the role of the visiting tutor is intended in some way to highlight any potential inconsistencies. The visiting tutors usually go to another school for an assessment and monitoring visit three times a year and the purpose is clearly understood ('*I go to schools and I go and see if the associate teacher is getting the support network they need at their individual school.*') Between these visits it is the colleague in each partnership school who has been designated as the senior link to the SCITT who oversees the quality assurance within that school. Kerry, the senior link tutor at Waterside, has a clear view of the evaluative processes that operate and the way in which the feedback obtained from the regular reviews is used to inform programme development. Many of those interviewed also highlight the need for the SCIITT to take account of the criteria informing any potential Ofsted inspection, and the latter is seen as an important aspect of the overall evaluation of the programme.

The PGCE mentors give differing views as to their own level of accountability for programme evaluation; while one sees this as being done collaboratively through discussion in mentor meetings at the university, the other PGCE mentor discusses only the feedback received from the student teacher in relation to the experiences of being mentored in the subject department. The professional tutor likewise sees her role in programme evaluation as only relating to those areas in which she has direct involvement – namely eliciting student teacher feedback focussed on the nature of the school placement experience.

The level of engagement with the range of ITE provision in the school

Overall, the school's engagement in teacher education both as a recently established SCITT and through ongoing involvement within an established HEI–school partnership is taken seriously and those responsible for the management of the SCITT in particular are keen to develop collaborative and responsive ways of working with their new school partners. What emerges very strongly from all the interviews conducted at Waterside is the way in which the positive response to involvement in teacher education, through either the SCITT or the more established partnership arrangements, is very much dependent on the calibre of certain individuals who are respected by colleagues for their expertise and commitment. Many of the mentors and subject specialists, for example, mention the way in which the SCITT director and the programme leaders listen carefully to colleagues' feedback and are responsive to it; there is consistent praise for the way in which Kerry, the SCITT senior link within the school, supports colleagues in their work with the associate teachers; individual subject specialists are seen to be serving a very valuable role in ensuring that the training provision is geared towards subject-specific pedagogy. There is a sense of collective endeavour, particularly in ensuring the efficient running of the SCITT, which is still a relatively new addition to the school's activities, and many of those involved talk about '*streamlining*' provision in order to make it increasingly effective. As the programme has evolved, a specific narrative appears to have developed, which affirms the value of this particular approach but which could also be seen to carry with it implied criticism of the models that existed previously. Terry, the SD salaried programme leader, says for example:

... the school-led approach is a way of finding teachers for their schools ... they get to see the reality of the school year ... they are very much viewed as members of the school as opposed to people who are arriving and disappearing.

(Terry, SD salaried programme leader)

Lisa, the SD fee-paying (non-salaried) programme leader, also implies that the programme is a better preparation for the realities of teaching:

The (associate teachers) have had a lot more time in schools compared to others, so for some people that is really quite useful, because otherwise it's a shock going into your NQT year. So it gets them ready for it.

(Lisa, SD fee-paying programme leader)

The majority of the school staff who have positions of responsibility within the SCITT are able to draw on their previous experience with established ITE partnerships and the majority of staff in these roles cite previous experience of collaboration within the pre-existing PGCE partnership. There are few apparent tensions between that ongoing partnership and the SCITT provision, and an acceptance that both can run concurrently. There appears, however, to be little evidence of any crossover between the two programmes and it is acknowledged that the two operate independently of each other. This sense of separation is evident in spite of both the previous close involvement of many of the key SCITT personnel with the established PGCE programme and the many concerns that they share in terms of programme effectiveness. For example, developing appropriate and relevant pedagogic approaches, ensuring that assessment practices are consistently rigorous yet at the same time able to support trainee teachers in their learning, supporting mentors in their work with associate teachers or student teachers, responding to the challenges of providing a programme in which teaching can be '*studied as well as practised*'.

IN A **NUTSHELL**

Waterside Academy has responded with energy and commitment to the policy agenda that emerged following the publication of the 2010 government White Paper, 'The Importance of Teaching'. It has built on its previous extensive and long-standing experience of working in partnership with a range of different HEIs to develop its own training provision and enthusiastically embraced the opportunities that have become available, particularly following its designation as a SCITT. The case study illustrates the confidence with which this work has been undertaken and the way in which key personnel have established a particular approach to teacher education within the school which is seen as being supportive, responsive to feedback and addressing local demand for the recruitment of new members of the teaching profession. This development has taken place alongside the school's ongoing involvement with one of its traditional HEI partners, with whom it has worked for over 30 years. The case study reveals the way in which different conceptualisations of the nature of ITE programmes are emerging with, perhaps, a greater emphasis being placed on the need for teachers to acquire first and foremost those skills that will equip them for the more immediate demands of the classroom and the realities they will face as newly qualified teachers.

REFLECTIONS ON **CRITICAL ISSUES**

The model of partnership being developed at Waterside Academy appears to be one that is fairly tightly controlled from the centre in terms of the way in which the programmes are both planned and evaluated, but it is also one which allows for some flexibility and more localised decision-making, where appropriate (either through provision within individual subject areas or through particular practices within partner schools). The importance of sufficiently rigorous quality assurance measures at all levels is acknowledged, but responsibility for ensuring that these are in place rests mainly with the school itself rather than being distributed across the partnership. The curriculum for both SD programmes (salaried and non-salaried) is focussed very much on developing knowledge and skills that can be applied immediately to the classroom context, with a view to having the beginning teachers, or associates, taking on responsibility for teaching their own classes at an earlier stage than might be the case for many PGCE programmes, including the one with which the school is also currently engaged. There is an acknowledgement that theory is important, but general agreement among the SCITT personnel that this should only come after the basics of classroom teaching have been mastered. Such a view appears to be accepted within the wider SCITT partnership of schools. Much of the success of the new model appears to rest on the expertise and commitment of staff involved in the management of the programme, who have been able to articulate a particular vision of school-based teacher education, which has, in turn, inspired confidence in all those with working within the programme.

CRITICAL **ISSUES**

- *What are the strengths of ITE partnership working?*
- *What are some of the perceived limitations?*
- *What knowledge and expertise is required to ensure that the curriculum can be delivered effectively?*
- *How do partnerships continue to develop and evolve as they mature?*

In addressing these issues we provide a detailed commentary on some of the key features of partnership working revealed by our examination of the Waterside Academy case study. We then use this analysis to raise questions about the ways in which partnerships have responded (and may continue to respond) to the significant changes in teacher education policy in England over recent years.

The perceived strengths of partnership working

The teachers at Waterside Academy who are involved in ITE operate either within the SCITT programme or the university PGCE programme, but rarely with both simultaneously. In each case these teachers were able to identify a number of strengths of working in ITE partnerships, some of which were common to both partnerships and some of which related more to one than to the other. Overall, the perceived areas of strength fall into a number of different categories:

- » the management structure of the programme;
- » the structure of the training programme itself;
- » the opportunities afforded to trainee teachers within the programme;
- » the way in which theory and practice are integrated;
- » the support available for trainees;
- » programme outcome factors.

The management structure

Effective management structures are seen as lying at the heart of the perceived strengths of both models of partnership, with particular value placed on good communication between partners. Easy access to those involved in leading the programme is also valued, particularly by those working within the SCITT, although it is acknowledged that such access may be more difficult for those working in schools in the wider SCITT partnership. In terms of overall management, the SCITT programme appears to be run essentially as a 'top-down' model, with most of the programme decision making coming from the director and the SD (non-salaried) and SD (salaried) programme leaders, but with responsibility for decisions as to how the subject-specific elements are delivered resting with the individual subject mentor. This is seen as a strength by those working within the programme:

It is what they call the central spine. And when I devised my training session I had to follow the central spine and adapt it to the (subject) needs and pedagogy, that sort of thing. So, it's been great to have the guidance.

(Caroline, SD mentor)

Kerry, the SD senior link, recognises, however, that the more devolved level of decision making within the university PGCE programme is a particular strength, with the aspiration within the SCITT to achieve such a model.

Regular evaluation of ITE programmes, which involves the whole partnership, is valued, in particular the capacity to respond quickly and appropriately to feedback, particularly from the trainee teachers themselves. The relatively small scale of the SCITT programme is seen as giving it the capacity to respond effectively:

The things that were fed back that weren't working have been changed. I do think that is one of our strengths as well – we are quite good at listening. Obviously you get the one or two that might just disagree with everything but in general things that weren't working ... tweaking them and making them better for next year.

(Lisa, SD fee-paying programme leader)

Likewise, programme evaluation is valued by the teachers as an important feature of the PGCE programme:

It's a collaborative thing between us mentors, the university and very much the trainees ... all of our targets are driven by their feedback at the end of the year when they say: 'actually, we felt that the programme was lacking in this area' and then that becomes one, that becomes a focus for us in looking forward.

(James, PGCE mentor)

One interesting aspect of partnership working identified through the case study was the level of engagement of headteachers in the process. One of the SCITT programme leaders expressed the view that being able to '*get directly to the heads as opposed to mentors who are often further down the chain*' is beneficial in terms of being able to deal with issues as and when they might arise. Those responsible for the management of the SCITT appeared to have stronger and more direct links with the headteachers in partnership schools than is perhaps the case with the university programme (where it is the mentors and the school's professional tutor who would have greater levels of engagement in any issues around programme management at a day-to-day level). This raises an interesting tension between the aspiration for ITE partnerships, on the one hand, to develop collaborative and distributed models of responsibility and, on the other hand, to be able to draw on existing hierarchies within schools to expedite management decisions in what is perceived to be the quickest and most effective way possible.

Another strength identified by the teachers at Waterside, related to overall management structures, is clarity in terms of programme procedures and expectations. Such clarity may be evident in relation to: the structure of the programme and the way in which it is designed to work; expectations of those working in particular roles within a given model; requirements for reporting the progress of trainees; and communication channels which enable information to be passed on quickly and efficiently.

The mentors within both models of partnership also highlight as a strength the quality of support and training that they receive, both the initial training and further mentor meetings throughout the year. In the SCITT model there are regular meetings (once a term) with the programme director or the programme leaders; the PGCE mentors meet four times a year with the university-based subject tutors in subject-specific groups. James, a PGCE mentor, sees this training as extending beyond what he requires in terms of supporting the PGCE students with whom he is working since it also provides him with opportunities for his own continuing professional development:

Although those meetings are ostensibly about how we better equip trainees, actually the big chunk of that meeting was us talking just as history teachers about how we might, how we might further our own kind of curriculum pedagogical knowledge ... and that certainly isn't atypical.

(James, PGCE mentor)

The structure of the training programme

The second broad area where strengths are identified is in relation to the structure of the training programme itself, albeit with some clear differences between the SCITT and the PGCE programmes but with each having a clear rationale for its respective structure and underpinning principles. For the mathematics and English subject specialists the SCITT partnership model is seen as being effective because it allows the associate teacher to be predominantly in one school for the duration of the training period and to begin the programme from the beginning of the school year in September. Furthermore, the SD (salaried) programme leader identifies the advantages in having the SD (salaried) associates begin their training before the start of the school year and then being in their main school from the beginning of September until mid-July (with experience in the second school taking place on one half-day per week over the course of the whole year). Dominic, a subject lead specialist, says that the associate teachers themselves prefer this model because *'they're just treated as a teacher'*. Although the PGCE programme also provides extensive experience in one setting for the majority of the training year, it takes a rather different approach since it seeks a balance in the first term between time spent at the university and time spent in schools. The professional tutor sees the latter as a strength of this particular partnership model:

I think the balance of starting with two days a week and going to three and then going to full time. I think that is really nice. I know there some students that feel 'Ah no, come on, we just want to teach.' But actually, I think they are wrong to think that. I think they need to realise that it's a difficult learning process and, if you are rushing, … you are probably not ready, and you probably do need to just think a bit harder about getting things sorted in your head as how you want to be as a teacher.

(Sonia, PGCE professional tutor)

Opportunities for trainees

A further factor relates to the status of the trainee teacher and the opportunities that this status affords them to gain access to a range of different teachers and different settings. While the SD (salaried) trainees are considered to be employees, the fee-paying (non-salaried) SD trainees are supernumerary (although the distinction between the two may not always be clear to other colleagues within the school). The PGCE students are, however, seen very clearly as colleagues engaged in the process of learning to teach and therefore not assigned sole responsibility for classes. Sonia points out that the PGCE model thus provides sufficient opportunities for the PGCE student to be observed regularly since there will always be a designated class teacher available to give feedback and to provide appropriate support and guidance. SCITT colleagues, however, identify the advantage in their programme of having a wide range of expertise distributed across the whole partnership (including both primary and secondary schools) on which associate teachers are able to draw. Additional learning opportunities can therefore be arranged flexibly in response to individual interests and needs. Paul, the SCITT director, sees this as a strength:

We draw on a whole range of schools because we operate within the Teaching School Alliance. We work with primary schools, specialist schools and secondary schools; we can therefore draw on expertise from across that … head teachers, senior leaders, subject leaders … from across that group of 200 schools. We're able to be therefore quite flexible in terms of how we establish placements. If individual trainees have particular interests in particular areas we are able to develop those and explore them further.

(Paul, SCITT director)

Integration of theory and practice

In terms of the relationship between theory and practice, there are clearly some differences in the underpinning philosophy of each of the respective ITE models operating at Waterside Academy. For those involved with the SCITT provision (covering both SD non-salaried and

SD salaried programmes) the lack of separation between theory and practice is viewed as a strength. The SCITT director is keen to establish and maintain overall coherence across all aspects of the training programme and contrasts this with his previous experiences of working within ITE partnerships:

One of the things that we are very keen to do from the outset, and a thing that I suppose I always found quite frustrating working with other providers prior to becoming one ourselves, is the disconnected nature sometimes of the central input and the school placements. So, you know, a key part of what we try and do is to make sure that those are integrated fully.

(Paul, SCITT director)

Terry, the SD salaried programme leader, is also highly conscious of the need for the programme to be relevant to the needs of beginning teachers and talks in detail about both the integration of policy and practice, as well as the role of theoretical ideas in the training programme. For him the value is in trainee teachers being able to see how an individual school is implementing policy and working with the actual practices of that school rather than dealing with a particular *'abstract concept'*. He acknowledges that it can be valuable for trainees to engage with both theoretical and practical perspectives in a synthesised way but suggests that this may not be valuable for many and may place too many demands on some. Being able to apply ideas for teaching and to get feedback immediately is something that Kerry also sees as a strength:

I like the interface between theory and practice by having the pedagogical input put in, in a school setting, so these things can be instantly applied, and teachers and trainers as well can figure out what works and what doesn't work, get quite immediate feedback on that.

(Kerry, SD senior link)

Nevertheless, Kerry also recognises a tension between the nature of her own PGCE programme and one which she valued, and that of the SCITT programme, notwithstanding the benefits that she had previously identified:

I did a PGCE course with Master's level credits, so the assignments that we did, just the level of reflection and analysis that that required, I think stood you in really good stead for your teaching career in general, and was also a mark of how intelligently you were required to do that job ... I think it does seem a little bit strange that you'd have people who are just in this kind of QTS only route. That's almost a bit more of an apprenticeship in teaching, and then your academic stuff might come later. For me, I think the two need to be combined.

Poppy, another SD mentor, has a very different view, based on her own training:

I think because it's School Direct, the trainees aren't necessarily wasting time ... well, not wasting time, but they're not having to do lots of days in uni and do lots of academic research ... when I did my PGCE I had to write a 5,000 word essay every term. So I think it's good that they don't have to do that, because they can actually focus on training and being in the lessons a lot more.

(Poppy, SD mentor)

For the SCITT mentors the key issue is that the trainees spend more time in the school setting, which provides 'hands-on' training as opposed to what is perceived as the more theoretical approach taken by university providers, whereas James argues that the university PGCE programme

takes the time to make sure that trainees understand the nuances – the kind of deep, deep understanding of what teaching history means, what teaching geography means, what teaching English means. I don't know they get that from other routes.

(James, PGCE mentor)

He also acknowledges, however, the way in which the SCITT places more emphasis on the trainee teacher as a practitioner (rather than as a learner) and sees this as a strength:

Look you do need to be learning, but first and foremost you are a professional. You're a professional and therefore you need to take responsibility for yourself… you need to take the initiative and make sure that you are on top of everything.

(James, PGCE mentor)

There are clearly some tensions between the two approaches yet these do not seem to affect the effective running of both models within the same school, and there is some sense that the strengths of each are valued by those working in the different programmes. Finally, there is recognition that trainees from different backgrounds and levels of experience may come with differing expectations of the nature of the training programme and may themselves see some aspects of the programme as being more relevant to their immediate needs than others.

Support for trainees

Furthermore there is agreement that trainees need to be well supported if they are to gain the most from their training. This support extends across all aspects of the trainees' work in school, encompassing the role of the mentor, support from other colleagues, pastoral support where appropriate and a particular focus on trainee teacher well-being. The level of support provided is seen as being linked to what Terry calls the *'buy-in'* of staff in the school and in the wider partnership, since their investment in terms of the time spent supporting trainees is seen to be worthwhile because many of the trainees will secure teaching posts at the schools in question at the end of the training period.

Programme outcomes

Finally, in terms of the programme outcomes, one of the factors identified at Waterside Academy is the need for trainees to be fully prepared for entering the profession as NQTs. There is a strong sense from the teachers involved in the SCITT programme in particular that being in school for longer makes their trainees better prepared for the NQT induction year since they will have, as James recognises, *'a real sense of autonomy and professional independence and professional kind of initiative'*. Nigel, one of the lead subject specialists, identifies that it is beneficial to have trainee teachers who are involved *'in the daily life of the school'* and who come to be seen no differently to other colleagues.

The perceived limitations and challenges of partnership working

Alongside the perceived strengths of the ITE partnerships at Waterside Academy, there is also an awareness of potential limitations to partnership working, which can be categorised in roughly similar ways:

» the management structure of the programme;

» the structure of the training programme itself;

» the way in which theory and practice are integrated;

» resource implications.

Management structures

The first of these limitations relates to the management structures of the SD programmes and in particular with the way in which the planning of the ITE programme (based on the common 'spine', which is produced by programme directors) may lead to more of a focus on generic rather than subject-specific aspects. A number of teachers highlight this as an issue, including Faith, a subject lead specialist, who says she has been *'frustrated'* because she would have preferred to deal with *'more specific (subject) issues but the central spine did not really allow for it'*. Caroline, the SD mentor in the same subject area, has similar views and sees an over-emphasis on *'generic skills for any teachers'* and Dominic, another lead specialist, concurs, in his expressed concern that the trainees are not getting enough *'specialist input'*. Terry, the SD salaried programme leader, acknowledges this lack as a potential problem, created by the need to accommodate *'different subjects each year'* and the lack of continuity in this respect, making it difficult to plan for the integration of subject-specific elements into the programme. Kerry, the senior link, also comments on the need for greater *'consistency of academic rigour across the subjects'*.

The structure of the training programme

The structure of the university PGCE programme is also seen to have its limitations, particularly with regard to the immediacy of communication possible within the SCITT structure and these limitations have implications for the structure of the training programme. James comments on the potential for a mismatch between the school and the university programmes when the latter requires a focus on *a different thing week by week and month by month and actually those two things will not always marry up with what we are doing in school and what actually I might look with my trainee, and say 'Well those really aren't your priorities actually, what you need to do, you should get this sorted'.*

(James, PGCE mentor)

Those responsible for the SCITT programmes have also been aware, as Val, an SD mentor in another subject points out, that there is a danger that the trainees did not, in the early days of the SCITT, *'necessarily understand the crossover between the central session and then how that applies in their classroom'*. She goes on to say that this has been addressed by introducing classroom-based tasks, which provide a link with the central training provision.

Issues around the timing of specific elements of the programme are also highlighted, emphasising the tension between programme coherence and continuity in terms of actual classroom teaching opportunities. While acknowledging the need for training that takes place outside the classroom many teachers comment on the potential disruption and discontinuity that this causes. The first term of the university PGCE programme, when time is divided each week between the university and the school, is seen as being unhelpful:

The way that they ask you to construct a timetable at two days a week and then three days a week is actually really bitty and doesn't help. It's not built, I don't think, from a school perspective.

(Simon, PGCE mentor)

Likewise the second school arrangements for trainees in the SD salaried programme, which involve half a day a week in the second school throughout the year, is seen to be disruptive to the continuity of the programme at Waterside. It is also criticised for failing to allow trainees to develop the necessary relationships and status within their second school since contact with the latter is so limited. There are also concerns expressed about the overall demands on the SD salaried trainees who may be considered more as employees than as trainees. As Terry notes, this status *'can sometimes compromise training'*. On the other hand the focus on the university PGCE students as learners is also problematic since it is seen as promoting a kind of dependency, not so evident with the SCITT trainees, which risks

... launching people into their NQT years, their first years as a qualified teacher without the level of autonomy and the kind of ability to self-govern.

(James, PGCE mentor)

Integration of theory and practice

Many of the teachers working at Waterside discussed the issues around the integration of theory and practice, particularly within the SCITT programmes, and Paul, the director, acknowledges this to be a potential limitation of any employment-based route in that *'there is not enough theory, and that it mistakes teaching for being something that you can do with an apprenticeship'*. For many of the teachers there appears to be a tension between an awareness of all the advantages that a school-based programme offers and the acknowledgement that trainees within such a programme may not have access to a sufficiently wide range of theoretical perspectives. Beatrice, an SD mentor, says there is a *'detachment of some kind of theory-based element'* and Kerry says that her aspiration is to have *'more academic input in central and subject based training'*.

Others talk about the way in which the issue can be addressed in a compensatory way (rather than necessarily focussing on greater levels of programme integration). Val appears to see both practice and theory as being essential elements of a training programme but ultimately not ones that are necessarily integrated. She suggests that the trainees could be provided with

... a library essentially of pedagogical information, current research, relevant stuff. Because actually while they're really, really good at developing practice and all the practical side of stuff, I'm not so sure they're as hot, because they don't do the essays in the same way, on the pedagogy and the ideology behind it.

(Val, PGCE mentor)

Lisa, the SD fee-paying programme leader, sees the opportunity to study for a PGCE qualification (offered by one of the local universities) as a way of compensating for any potential deficit in the school-based programme because *'we don't want them to miss out on that educational research side'*.

Similar concerns about the effective integration of theory and practice are highlighted in relation to the university PGCE programme, whose student teachers may come into school with unrealistic ideas. Dominic, a SD subject mentor, sees this reflected in a tension between teaching 'innovative' and 'traditional' lessons, and feels that the SD trainees accept more readily that the latter are a necessary part of their overall repertoire. Kerry summarises the wider tensions inherent in perceptions of different types of training programme and the ultimate aspiration to address such tensions:

... and I think a really good mix of academic rigour so that your (trainee teachers) *are thinking really deeply, but also up to date expertise in schools, because everybody's ideal I think is that hybrid model of those two things. So in all the models I've worked with, I don't think I've seen like a perfect blend of those two things, but that's what everybody aspires to I guess.*

(Kerry, SD senior link)

Resource implications

Given that Waterside has primarily led the development of the SCITT programmes and provided a significant number of the subject specialists across the wider partnership of schools there have been specific resource implications for the school. While the staff speak enthusiastically about the training programme and the opportunities that it offers, there is also an acknowledgement that the development of the SCITT has brought with it an increasing workload. Val summarises her dilemma in wanting to give more time to supporting the associate teachers, but recognising the compromises involved in doing so:

I don't necessarily see my associate teacher as much as I'd like to. Things slip under the net in a big way and then suddenly ... rather than dealing with things as they come up, it's kind of crisis management at certain points, because you haven't had those chances to check in. Or it just means if you try and go the other way and you invest lots of time in your associate, your own classes suffer, because you're not doing as much planning or as much marking or the things that you need to do for your day-to-day job.

(Val, SD mentor)

Knowledge and expertise

ITE partnerships need to provide trainee teachers with the opportunity to draw on a range of sources of knowledge and to have access to appropriate expertise throughout their training, although the way in which this is achieved may vary from partnership to partnership. Such variation is particularly apparent when comparing more traditional models (usually involving an HEI provider and a range of school partners) to those operating within SCITTs. The Waterside Academy case study indicates that the school-based staff responsible for planning and delivering the teacher training programme in the school are able to draw on five kinds of professional knowledge or experience:

» recollections of the experience of their own initial training;

» their knowledge and expertise as a teacher;

» the individual teacher's previous experience and current role as a teacher educator;

» their contextual knowledge as established members of the school community;

» subject knowledge.

Teachers' recollections of their own initial training

First, the teacher's recollections of their own initial training represent an important point of reference and play an important role in shaping their understanding of the trainee teachers' needs. Often they enable those working with trainee teachers to be empathetic when dealing with the challenges that those trainees now face. At Waterside Academy this was evident from the teachers involved in both training programmes. The professional tutor involved with the university programme, Sonia, draws on one negative aspect of her own training experience to recognise that that there are inevitably *'issues with personality clashes that can be tricky'*. Nigel, one of the subject lead specialists within the SCITT, sees the current experience of the SD trainees as being similar to what he himself experienced as a trainee teacher (within the previous Graduate Teacher Programme in England): required to meet *'the challenges of being almost thrown into the school setting and having to cope with the higher teaching workload initially and combine that with the theoretical input*. Beatrice, one of the SD mentors, even refers back to the reading she had been given during her training, which she now re-evaluates in light of her subsequent experience as a teacher: '*I can see how that now works in a school situation*'.

Teacher knowledge and expertise

Second, those involved draw on their knowledge and expertise as a teacher. Confidence in her role as a teacher, following ten years of teaching experience, leads Sonia to feel in a strong position to be '*able to pass on advice to other people*'. One of the other teachers, Caroline, says that her own ongoing professional development as a teacher has equipped her to carry out the role of mentor more effectively and Nigel says that being reflective in his own practice has enabled him '*to apply some of those same ideas to when I'm working with trainees*'. Conversely, those with less teaching experience and who are, perhaps, more con-scious of their lack of knowledge and expertise in certain areas, tend to see their role as a teacher educator differently. Beatrice, who is in her third year of teaching and in her second year at Waterside Academy, indicates that she relies very much on the central organisa-tion and the core structures of the SD programme in order to guide her as to how she approaches her work both as a mentor and as a subject specialist within the SCITT. She is aware that her lack of experience as a teacher means that she is still exploring the rationales for her own practice and she is therefore happy to follow a prescribed ITE programme that does not require her to consider for herself the approaches that she might wish to take:

And they are just really clear what you need to do, so I kind of know ... I have been given the list of things that we need to cover and they are like 'this is what you need to do, here, here, here and here, any problems let us know'.

(Beatrice, SCITT mentor)

Previous experience and current role

Third, the individual teacher's previous experience and current role as a teacher educator also appears to be an important factor, with Paul, the SCITT programme director, acknow-ledging that the '*... accumulation of knowledge and experience over time is vital*'. In his case he cites '*twenty odd years of being in schools and being involved with teacher training ...*' and being able to draw on the various networks of which he is a member, particularly those related directly to teacher training. Terry, the SD salaried programme leader, like-wise draws on his past experience of ITE and says that in particular his '*... work at the university as first a mentor and second a part-time curriculum tutor was really influential*'. Similarly, Simon, a mentor with the PGCE programme, highlights the value of his previous experiences working with trainee teachers, which have taught him that '*we need to allow them that time to develop*'. Experience within the role develops over time but also benefits from specific professional training. Nigel, for example, cites the professional development opportunities that come from being involved in the SCITT programme, such as receiving training in how to design and lead an effective adult learning session. James, a PGCE mentor, talks about the value of working closely with colleagues at the university and this is seen very much as a two-way process: not only does it enable the mentors to support the trainee teachers effectively but it also has a beneficial effect on the teachers' own classroom practice. He provides the example of a meeting at the university between subject tutors and mentors, which focussed on the use of online resources and historical archives, and which had multiple benefits since

while the kind of direction was about how we can support trainees to do this, actually it is invaluable to us because we spend half an hour just talking about how we can incorporate historical articles into our lessons …

(James, PGCE mentor)

Faith also explains how her responsibilities within the programme have enriched her own professional development since it has been necessary for her, in her role as a subject lead specialist and visiting tutor, to do a lot of reading in order '… *to try and explore areas of pedagogy … I was supposed to deliver on, so I have done a lot of reading which has enriched my job'*. Not all of those involved, however, have had direct experience of ITE previously; three of the teachers at Waterside Academy who were interviewed as part of the data collection for the case study (Val, Poppy and Beatrice) had had no such experience and were perhaps more reliant on the expertise and support of their more experienced colleagues, as well as on the information contained within the course documentation.

Contextual knowledge

School-based teacher educators are also able to draw on detailed contextual knowledge as members of the school community. This contextual knowledge is wide-ranging, incorporating knowledge of the school itself and the wider community in which it is situated, knowledge of a range of teaching approaches in the school, knowledge of the pupils and knowledge of where the expertise is distributed across the school in relation to delivering specific areas of the ITE curriculum. Those responsible for drawing up the timetables for trainee teachers, particularly in the early stages when they may be spending a greater proportion of their time observing experienced teachers, need to know which teachers are the strongest practitioners in relation to specific areas.

Subject knowledge

Strong subject knowledge is also identified as an important requirement for those supporting the learning of trainee teachers in the school, by which they mean not simply knowledge of the subject itself but also (or perhaps more importantly) of specific subject pedagogy. Those responsible for the subject dimension of the SCITT programme clearly see the importance of providing an appropriate curriculum. Nigel, one of the subject lead specialists, talks about collaborating with another subject specialist in order to '*put together what we felt was the best way of interpreting the central training spine for (the subject)'*. Others value the opportunities they have had to develop their subject knowledge and subject pedagogy, which have stood them in good stead for their teacher education roles. Simon, one of the PGCE mentors, talks about an externally funded secondment opportunity, which enabled him to focus on his subject teaching. Kerry, the SD senior link at Waterside, speaks positively about the continuing professional development (CPD) opportunities that the school has funded, including her study towards a Masters qualification, which included a strong subject-specific element; she also talks about the advantages of being familiar with '*the latest research or trends in teaching, and developing or adding to our existing training sessions ... and selecting readings for the associates to use*'.

What knowledge and expertise is seen by school-based teacher educators as being required within an ITE partnership?

In addition to the knowledge and expertise that the teachers bring to the programme, they also talk about what is necessary in order for them to be able to fulfil their school-based teacher educator roles effectively. Paul, the SD programme director, regards it as essential to have '*expert practitioners sharing their expertise with trainees*'. The identification of key elements of a successful programme tend, however, to be expressed less in terms of knowledge and expertise and more in relation to programme structures, curriculum organisation and overall teacher dispositions.

One aspect of this is the view that the core documentation needs to be clear and a number of teachers working in the SCITT programme highlight clarity in this respect as one of its most important strengths. Val, one of the SD mentors, is appreciative of the fact that, for her, the handbook represents '*the stuff that you absolutely need to know*' and others talk about the way in which the course documentation provides a clear overview of the structure of the programme and the way in which each of the component parts relates to the central 'spine'. Additionally it was felt to be advantageous to have consistent pro-formas, used across the whole SCITT partnership, with exemplars in the handbook of how these might be completed.

The professional context in which the teachers are working is also seen as being important in terms of the capacity of the programme to provide effective training. This encompasses a range of elements, not merely the presence of individual teachers recognised as being outstanding classroom practitioners, but a commitment to ongoing professional learning and the provision of sufficient professional development opportunities, all overseen by a strong leadership team. Lisa, the SD fee-paying leader, highlights the advantage of having '*people within schools that have real passion for teaching and learning*'.

Effective leadership of the teacher education programme is likewise seen as an essential prerequisite – that is to say programme managers who are well respected for their expertise as teachers but who are also knowledgeable about ITE itself and understand how to support the development of their colleagues' expertise as teacher educators. Poppy, another SD mentor, is clear that '*in order to be a good mentor, you need to have a good senior link*', and Kerry, the SD senior link, in turn talks about needing to be good herself at '*managing difficult conversations or helping support people when there are issues*'.

Finally, what might be called the 'human dimension' is highlighted as being important in that school-based teacher educators have to be able to support adult learners, which may require a different set of skills to those required for teaching younger learners. Terry, the SD salaried programme leader, talks about the need to take account of the trainee teacher as a learner and to be both flexible and supportive throughout. He says that it is important that schools are willing

to lead trainees through difficult times and make adjustments, be it timetabling, be it staff they are working with, be it the amount they expect from those trainees; to make adjustments in order to get a successful teacher out of it.

(Terry, SD salaried programme leader)

Overall, therefore, the essential prerequisites (as expressed by teachers working as teacher educators within SCITT) appear to be programme leaders who have the expertise and capacity to support the day-to-day work and further development of those working as mentors and subject leads who are, in turn, able to provide direct support and guidance for the trainee teachers themselves. These support mechanisms need to be underpinned by clear structures and systems which enable the training to be operationalised successfully, including the use of clear and commonly understood documentation.

Partnership development

The SCITT partnership model at Waterside Academy sees itself as continuing to evolve, with those involved in the programme identifying two main areas of development:

» consultation, collaboration and communication between partners;
» mentoring expertise across the partnership.

Consultation, collaboration and communication

Consultation, collaboration and effective communication are understood at Waterside to be vital features of an effective partnership model. The way in which those managing the training programme have been able to respond quickly to any feedback (from all sources) is highlighted by many of those interviewed who note that this quick action has led to notice-able improvements over time. There is an acknowledgement that, in the initial stages, certain aspects were not operating effectively, but effective systems of monitoring and evaluation have ensured that the necessary development has taken place. Nigel sees this as being an ongoing, formative process:

I think every year they're putting a huge amount of work into consulting the specialists, the visiting tutors, the trainees, and harvesting feedback and using that to implement them better, in a way a better programme next year.

(Nigel, SD subject lead)

Kerry, the senior link within the school for the SCITT programme, draws on her previous experience of working as a professional tutor within the university PGCE programme to highlight the benefits of having an effective consultation:

I think we're trying to work towards now a much more consultative model where we regularly check in with our partners on all levels, so mentors, senior links, visiting teachers, everyone involved in the process, which has been interesting, because on the PGCE programme I think – when I worked on that – that's a massive strength because it's highly consultative, so all of the partners feel very valued and they feel that they have a genuine input into things, rather than a kind of tokenistic, 'Oh what do you think?' after a decision's already been made.

(Kerry, SD senior link)

The SCITT director also sees communication between partners as being a necessary strength, and highlights the 'sense of collaboration' between partners at all levels (and specifically in the initial selection of trainees, where schools play a significant role). He sees consultation as taking place both 'widely' and 'regularly' but with a particular focus on the management of the training programme and its ongoing evaluation. There appears, however, to be less emphasis on consultation and collaboration in respect of the planning of the curriculum itself, which tends to be led more by those with responsibility within the SCITT, as Kerry points out:

... it's mainly the programme leaders and the SCITT director who decide the curriculum content, and subject specialists obviously have their input as well.

(Kerry, SD senior link)

James, a university PGCE mentor at Waterside, talks about the value of the '*real dialogue that exists between the university and us as mentors*' but also highlights the way in which this dialogue relates also to subject-specific curriculum planning.

Those involved in both programmes highlight the value of effective communication (both written and oral, although predominantly the latter), although the way in which communication is talked about does differ from individual to individual and appears to focus on two key aspects – accessibility and clarity. In terms of communicating with programme managers, those involved in the SCITT programme value the accessibility of colleagues and the structures that enable frequent dialogue, but again it has to be acknowledged that these are colleagues working in the same school and that such accessibility might be more difficult to maintain across the wider partnership involving a range of different schools. Those involved with the PGCE course acknowledge that face-to-face meetings are usually limited to designated mentor meetings (four times a year) or curriculum tutor visits to schools (four times a year) unless there are specific issues, but James suggests that there is '*a lot of almost expected telepathy between us*', which could be interpreted as a strength (in that expectations are jointly agreed and operationalised) or a weakness (in that there is insufficient personal contact). Clarity is likewise understood to be important, particularly with reference to the management structures within the SCITT. Current practice is seen to have developed as a result of increased clarity in terms of both expectations and the way in which information about the programme itself is communicated to all participants (including through the programme handbooks) within the SCITT management structure. Several of those interviewed comment on the necessity for effective communication given the nature of a teacher's working life.

One wider aspect of collaboration and communication at Waterside relates to the existence of two different ITE programmes operating simultaneously alongside each other. In this respect the two schemes appear to run independently of each other with little crossover between the two. Kerry, the senior link, puts this down more to individual personalities and preferred ways of working rather than to any fundamental systemic differences, commenting that the school's professional tutor Sonia *'works in a much more compartmentalised way than me'*. Although the role of the professional tutor within the university programme might be compared in some ways to the senior link role within the SCITT, the latter encompasses wider responsibilities (such as reporting formally on trainee progress six times a year and initiating and monitoring the procedures put into place when a trainee is designated as being a cause for concern) with the result that the senior link role is one which is understood to be more time consuming. While the two schemes clearly operate in very different ways it is nevertheless interesting that there is no single overarching structure at Waterside that brings both of them together at any level, even though the SCITT programme clearly relies on the expertise developed through previous involvement in the university PGCE programme. The model appears to be one of separation rather than one of ongoing knowledge exchange. It may be that the apparent lack of continuing cross-fertilisation of ideas has been due to the need to create a distinct identity for the SCITT, or perhaps due to the lack of time available for effective liaison between those working within the two schemes, but, as the new partnership continues to evolve, it is perhaps worth asking whether it might be worth deliberately seeking to promote approaches that would perhaps better support continued learning *across* the two schemes (given the school's continued engagement in both).

Mentoring expertise

Developing effective mentors might be one potential focus for such shared learning, given the acknowledged importance of consistency in the quality of mentoring for any ITE partnership and given that the development of mentoring expertise across the partnership is an ongoing feature of the SCITT's work. Paul, the director, sees effective mentoring as *'expert practitioners sharing that expertise with trainees'* and that while he is confident that this occurs at Waterside Academy, he wants to establish and maintain

really high quality and consistency in our partner schools in terms of mentoring and support so the provision that they get there is as good as the provision that they get here.

(Paul, SCITT director)

He sees this as equipping mentors with appropriate leadership skills and providing an appropriate framework within which they can work as mentors. Lisa, the the SD fee-paying leader, emphasises the need for a consistent approach and clarity of *'key messages'* to mentors and Terry, the SD salaried programme leader, gives an example of this in highlighting the fact that recent developments have necessitated *'teaching our assessment processes to the mentors and the senior links that are involved'*. Kerry acknowledges this tension and identifies that

the training sessions that we've had over the last couple of years have had to be very process driven and instructional, because there's a whole new set of assessment criteria and processes and job roles and titles to get your head round. But I think what's lacking is really high quality training on mentoring skills, so I'm actually working on that as a project at the moment to try and get really high-quality mentoring skills out to schools so we're not doing all of that just three times a year in the meetings.

(Kerry, SD senior link)

IN A **NUTSHELL**

Waterside is an interesting case study in that it works with a university provider as part of a long-established partnership and yet, as a result of the opportunities provided by policy reforms in England from 2010 onwards, the school has also developed its own ITE programmes and gained accreditation as a SCITT provider. Interviews with key personnel involved in both partnerships reveal little overlap between the two models within the school but an acceptance that each has its strengths. There is, however, a keen awareness among all those involved of the emphasis within the SCITT programmes on the focus of the training being for a specific context: that is to say, those completing the programme are likely to work in the school in which they have been trained, or at least in a school in the local area. As a result it could be argued that there is less encouragement for trainees to take a critical stance on the policies and practices of the schools in which they are being trained, resulting in a predominantly 'craft' model. It is nevertheless recognised that partnerships do need to be able to provide as wide a range of perspectives as possible to support trainee teachers' learning and that, for secondary trainees in particular, the development of subject pedagogy has to be an essential feature of the training programme. The question that remains, however, is the extent to which any partnership is able to integrate a range of different perspectives (both theoretical and practical) in order to develop overall programme coherence.

REFLECTIONS ON **CRITICAL ISSUES**

ITE partnerships are strong when there is clarity of purpose and shared aims agreed with all those involved in the planning, delivery and evaluation of the programme, along with effective management structures and decision-making processes. The latter may be based on more hierarchical or more distributed models but in either case there has to be trust from those working within the model that effective decisions are made which further the overall programme aims. There are some perennial issues within partnerships, whatever their constitution, which are often focussed on sufficient resources being available and, a related concern, on the consistency of the quality of mentoring across the partnership. Key to the success of any ITE partnership is its ability to draw on a range of knowledge and expertise, reflecting the complex knowledge base required for teaching itself, but there may be challenges if the partnership does not have the capacity to offer sufficiently diverse perspectives to enable trainee teachers to evaluate their practice in an appropriately critical way. The question as to how partnerships develop and evolve can be answered in different ways. One approach might be for a particular partnership to focus on consolidating further the structural elements of the programme that it sees as being its core strengths (and which may be aspects that distinguish it from other similar partnerships) in order to empha-sise its distinctiveness. An alternative approach might be to seek to address some of the wider challenges of ITE partnership working (see, for example, the discussion of teacher education pedagogy in Chapter 1) and particularly the need to ask critical questions of accepted practices in the specific context in which trainees are placed. This would, however, require a willingness to grapple with the inevitable tensions arising from any consideration of alterna-tive approaches.

CRITICAL **ISSUES**

- *What are the inherent tensions and challenges within particular ITE partnership models?*
- *What are the underlying principles that might inform any partnership model?*
- *How might these principles be reflected in practice?*
- *What are the critical questions that partnerships need to ask?*

The tensions and challenges within ITE partnerships

The case study presented in the previous chapters highlights a number of features of teacher education provision within what might be considered a new model of partnership, developed primarily as a result of the significant policy changes in England since 2010 (outlined in Chapter 1). Such a model needs to be understood in the context of what policy-makers at the time saw as the lack of relevance and suitability of existing programmes and partnership models which were judged to be more HEI-led than collaborative, and in which schools were seen to have insufficient involvement in respect of trainee recruitment, ITE curriculum design, programme delivery and the assessment of trainee outcomes. Waterside Academy, along with its wider local Teaching School Alliance, took the opportunity to develop its own ITE programme and to provide training within the School Direct model and to establish its own SCITT. In many ways the ITE policy landscape in England has changed so radically that analyses of previous forms of partnership working may now be of limited relevance. Nevertheless, it is worth considering the case of Waterside Academy in light of the tensions and challenges identified in Chapter 2, and to examine the extent to which they are evident in this new type of partnership model. The tensions identified were:

1. partners may not necessarily share the same conceptualisation of what constitutes effective teacher preparation;

2. there may be tensions between the differing goals of preparing a teacher to be 'school ready' or 'profession-ready';

3. partners have differing priorities and differing levels of accountability;

4. schools often engage in complex partnership arrangements with different ITS providers.

1. Partners may not necessarily share the same conceptualisation of what constitutes effective teacher preparation

The evidence from Waterside would seem to indicate that divergent views of effective teacher preparation do not present an issue for those who work within the SCITT programme. The ethos that underpins the whole programme is a pragmatic one in that the programme is preparing teachers who are expected to work in the specific local contexts in which they are training. The overall focus is on ensuring that those being trained are fully equipped with the classroom skills necessary for them to navigate with relative ease the transition to their first post as an NQT. Staff at the school speak variously about the way in which the programme develops autonomy, independence, resilience, initiative and a sense of realism.

For those working within the university PGCE programme there is, however, more evidence of the tension mentioned. While recognising the importance of the programme's focus on requiring the trainee teachers to draw on a range of sources (both theoretical and practical) to inform their developing thinking and practice, there is nevertheless a sympathy among some of the PGCE subject mentors with the SCITT approach, which is seen to be more focussed on classroom-based experience.

Overall the evidence would suggest that in new models of partnership, such as this one, it is the craft model of teaching that underpins the training programme and, as Brown et al (2015) note, the dominant approach is of *'conceptions of practice that integrate situated conceptions of theory responsive to the needs of practice'* (2015, p 5). Such a model might be seen to be somewhat limited in contrast to a wider conceptualisation of teacher professionalism (see, for example, Winch et al, 2015) in which teachers' practice is informed by research at all levels.

2. There may be tensions between the differing goals of preparing a teacher to be *school ready* or *profession-ready*

As mentioned above, the SCITT programme is focussed on preparing teachers to work within a specific context and the views of the teachers involved as to what might count as success in terms of trainee outcomes are generally in line with that expressed by Val:

And it's really rewarding when there's somebody who comes out and then you give them a job, because you've nurtured them and fostered them and then they fit into the school and that's really, really nice.

(Val, SD mentor, English)

The primary focus is on preparing teachers for local schools within which they will follow the established practices, and some teachers explicitly state that it is not helpful to have trainees who may want to introduce innovative methods into their teaching. Dominic, the SD mathematics mentor, criticises the *'new and innovative is good – old is bad'* approach (which he says characterises the way that PGCE student teachers tend to think) and sees the 'what works from the old and from the new and using it' approach (which he says characterises the SD trainees) as being more pragmatic and beneficial.

There are thus few tensions within the SCITT programme around its underpinning goals and the way in which training leads to these goals being realised, although there is little acknowledgement also of the need to develop what might be called 'adaptive expertise' (Berliner, 2001). Such expertise is, it could be argued, necessary in order to provide these beginning teachers with the capacity to draw on a wide range of knowledge and experience and to use this expertise to deal with problems or issues that may be encountered in any different context in the future. Overall the tendency to equip trainees to deal with the immediacy of their current context may risk the danger of 'preparing beginning teachers for the status quo' (McIntyre, 2009, p 603) or of 'teaching by proxy' (Edwards and Protheroe, 2004, p 183), that is, a tendency for mentors to expect their trainees to teach in exactly the same way as they would were they themselves to be taking the lesson.

While one of the stated aims of the university PGCE programme may be to equip its student teachers for career-long professional learning and while this is recognised as being important by the teachers directly involved with the programme, there remain some tensions as to how this is best realised, particularly when time spent at the university is seen as potentially disrupting school-based learning opportunities. Overall, however, there is agreement that those entering the profession do need to have knowledge of a wider range of perspectives than those which are experienced in the context of just one school.

3. Partners have differing priorities and differing levels of accountability

Working with different models of partnership within the same school inevitably leads to comparisons being made. The most significant difference relates inevitably to where the responsibility for each individual programme lies, and since the SCITT programme at Waterside is essentially managed by the school itself there are fewer tensions than if the programme were being managed elsewhere. The SCITT director, the SD programme directors and many of the subject specialists and visiting tutors are existing members of the school's staff and the management hierarchy reflects the wider school staffing structures (the SCITT director is one of the school's assistant headteachers and those with other more senior responsibilities within the programme have experience as head of subject departments or as professional development coordinators in the school; mentors are experienced classroom teachers). Channels of communication and line management structures are therefore already established internally and accepted, so there is potentially less resistance than might be the case if the direction of the programme is coming from an 'external' partner. The immediacy of the partnership and the close involvement in it of colleagues who are at the same time engaged in teaching pupils in the school on a day-to-day basis does seem to give a sense of everybody working together with common goals. Furthermore, although resourcing is highlighted as an issue and in particular the time required to mentor the trainee teachers effectively, there is a recognition that those responsible for directing the programme are aware of such issues and are responsive, wherever possible, to mentors and to others involved in the delivery of the SCITT programme. Central to this responsiveness appears to be the strength of the relationships that are built up and a certain level of trust, often based on existing established relationships within the school, but again it may be that colleagues working within the partnership schools without this level of immediacy may think differently.

4. Schools often engage in complex partnership arrangements with different ITE providers

As a result of policy changes at national level Waterside has been able to seize the opportunity to become more actively involved in the training of teachers through becoming an accredited SCITT provider in its own right, yet it has continued to work with the local university PGCE programme and to maintain this partnership, which was established over 30 years ago. In many ways the tensions that could arise when schools work within multiple-partnerships (Mutton and Butcher, 2008) are not evident at Waterside because there are only two parallel ITE programmes at the school, each of which is operated separately. Subject departments within the school may host trainees from one programme or the other, or even both at the same time, but if it is the latter then this will be with a separate mentor, and separate professional tutor or senior link as appropriate.

The key feature of the SCITT is that all its operating mechanisms are internal to the school so there is little *'boundary crossing'* (Edwards and Mutton, 2007) with all of the complexities that this entails. What is less clear, however, is the extent to which such complexity is manifest within the wider SCITT partnership, although it could be surmised that since this is a school-led approach with 'buy-in' from local headteachers and their colleagues, there are likely to be fewer tensions than if the direction of the programme were coming from what might be perceived as a more distant partner such as a university. What is clear, however, is that Waterside, as the lead school within the SCITT, has decided to manage the potential complexity of working with two different programmes by generally keeping both separate, with staff involved in either one or the other, but not usually both (unless individual class teachers happen to be working with trainees from both schemes across different classes). While the emphasis on clear communication and core documentation within the SCITT is partly informed by the need to distinguish the two partnerships, there is nevertheless some acknowledgment that it is difficult for staff who are not involved as mentors to understand what should be expected of trainees following different programmes.

The underlying principles for partnerships

Having considered a range of issues in relation to ITE partnership working and examined how national policy is being implemented within one specific school context we will now set out a series of principles which we believe could be usefully applied to a number of different models of ITE. These principles take into account the existing ITE partnership literature but have been designed to reflect equally the way in which partnerships are being developed and managed within the current policy context, informed by the Waterside

Academy case study discussed earlier. We therefore want to present these as a series of *pragmatic* principles, which are equally relevant to both traditional models of school–HEI partnerships and to well-established, or more recently accredited, SCITT providers.

Principle 1: Partnerships need to have clear agreement in terms of the programme aims (and specifically a shared view of what the desired trainee outcomes should be)

While it might be assumed that there are common underlying goals to all ITE partnership working, this may not always necessarily be the case. While all ITE programmes in England have to be compliant with a number of statutory requirements, set out in the *'Initial teacher training: criteria for providers'* (DfE and NCTL, 2017) and are also expected to be aligned with the *'Core content framework for ITE'* (DfE, 2016a) in the way in which they prepare trainee teachers to meet the Teachers' Standards (DfE, 2011c), there is no requirement to adopt any one specific approach to professional learning. Different models of partnership may be informed by differing pedagogical principles and, within any given partnership, different partners may share differing views as to what beginning teachers, by the end of the period of their training, need to know and be able to do. The former is less problematic if, within each individual partnership, the underlying aims are explicitly articulated and agreed. In the case of the SCITT programme at Waterside Academy this is clearly the case with the emphasis being placed on the effective preparation of teachers who will be able subsequently to make the transition easily to employment as an NQT within one of the partnership schools. In programmes where there may be greater emphasis placed on developing beginning teachers' capacity to engage in the process described variously as *'clinical reasoning'* (Kriewaldt and Turnidge, 2013) or *'practical theorising'* (McIntyre, 1993; Hagger and McIntyre, 2006), as is the case with the university programme with which Waterside Academy also works in partnership, it may not be as easy to achieve, across the whole partnership, the necessary level of collective engagement with programme aims. Such approaches, which require trainee teachers to draw on a range of different sources, both theoretical and practical, involve a *'process of hypothesis-testing, requiring interpretation and judgment in action, rather than the routinised application of learned repertoires'* (Burn and Mutton, 2013, p 4) and may be considered by many teachers, as illustrated in the Waterside case study, to represent something best seen as an optional extra, rather than as a central aspect of the training programme itself. It could be argued, however, that one way to minimise potential differences of this sort is to ensure that there is a clearly defined learning programme.

Principle 2: Partnerships need a clearly defined learning programme in order for their trainee teachers to be able to capitalise fully on their school-based experiences

It may be very tempting, particularly in the context of the development of employment-based routes into teaching, for partnerships to focus predominantly on the classroom performance of trainee teachers – especially when these trainees take on whole class teaching responsibilities at an early stage – and to see the process of learning to teach as being one that might best be described as an apprenticeship. Within such a model there is, however, a danger that the ITE curriculum then becomes more focussed on *doing* than on *learning,* which is why the needs of trainees as learners need to be recognised through the provision of a curriculum or learning programme, which ensures that they have sufficient time both to learn how to plan and to evaluate their teaching experiences effectively (Burn et al, 2015). The latter requires them to draw on a range of sources of evidence (see later) in order to develop the necessary criteria by which to reflect on their recent experiences in the classroom and is an integral part of a carefully planned programme that is structured to take account of the needs of the beginning teachers themselves.

The SCITT partnership based at Waterside Academy has such a programme designed to meet the learning needs of its trainees, although it does vary significantly from the university PGCE programme, which also operates within the same school. The five-week SCITT pre-course 'summer programme' aims, according to the course handbook, to provide '*rapid immersion in theoretical and practical skills and an understanding of essential elements for successful classroom practice*' while the school-based training sessions during the year aim to '*develop theoretical and practical skills and understanding of the elements of successful classroom practice and the broader roles and responsibilities of being a teacher as set out in the Teachers' Standards*', although the focus of the training sessions relates primarily to more generic aspects of teaching, such as assessment, behaviour management and some aspects of learner motivation. There is nevertheless a clearly defined structure for subject specialists to take forward the ideas from the core provision in relation to subject-specific contexts, and also guidance for mentors to encourage the trainees to reflect regularly on their experiences of teaching. Furthermore, many of those interviewed commented on the benefits of trainees being able to draw on the expertise of a range of experienced teachers across the partnership who are recognised for the quality of their teaching.

The challenge for devising any ITE programme lies in maintaining a balance between two competing tensions: on the one hand not wanting trainees to feel overwhelmed by the scope of what they need to learn (in order to be adequately prepared for the '*multidimensionality*' and '*unpredictability*' (Doyle, 1977) with which they will inevitably be faced) and on the other hand, acknowledging that the nature and complexity of what needs to be learnt mean that it cannot easily be packaged as units within a neatly structured programme. Furthermore, trainees may tend to value more highly the training that they perceive as having immediate, rather than longer-term applicability. The programme therefore has to be both comprehensive in scope, yet responsive in terms of the trainees' current needs and priorities, so that work-based learning is '*structured as much as is necessary to maximize learners' cognitive access to the full normal realities of doing the work, but must not distort these realities*' (Hagger and McIntyre, 2006, pp 49–50).

Finally, as we have argued elsewhere (Hagger et al, 2008), it has to be understood that the capacity for beginning teachers to learn from experience is likely to be limited if they are not able to draw on as wide a range of sources as possible, including both the expertise of those within the ITE partnership, which is training them, as well as wider research and scholarship. One further important source is the learners themselves – the pupils the trainees are actually teaching. Interestingly only one of the interviewees (Caroline) comments on the value of learning from one's own pupils, and then only in relation to her own ongoing learning as a teacher, but understanding the learners' perspective can be hugely beneficial to a trainee teacher's development, something which may be easily overlooked when the focus is primarily on the need for trainees to gain as much classroom experience as possible. Poppy reflects this focus when she says: '*I think the best way to get good at something is to do it as much as you can*' but the view that *doing* is enough to secure *learning* can be seen to be problematic. While sustained periods of classroom practice are likely to enable beginning teachers to develop a basic level of competence as classroom teachers, wider opportunities within the ITE curriculum are also necessary if they are to be equipped with the expertise and habits necessary for critically evaluating their ongoing and developing practice.

Principle 3: Partnerships need to consider when and how their trainees will develop the adaptive expertise necessary for sustaining a career in teaching

Berliner (2001), in defining the nature of adaptive expertise, argues that '*expert, domain-specific contextualized knowledge can often be a limited kind of knowledge*' (2001, p 473) and that the expertise required for teaching entails being able to relate new situations, as they are encountered, to an existing knowledge base. In developing the idea further, Hammerness et al (2005) point out that while teachers need to be efficient in '*acquiring and using well-learned schemas and routines*' (2005, p 374) they also need to balance this efficiency with the ability to innovate, that is to say, '*to move beyond existing routines… to rethink key ideas, practices, and even values*' (pp 358–359) in order to be able to respond to new situations they will encounter in the future. Both efficiency and the capacity to innovate, the authors argue, need to be learned alongside each other and they put forward a framework for teacher learning, which necessitates a complex interplay between a range of four key areas:

> » understanding (ie a deep knowledge of content, pedagogy, students and social contexts);
>
> » practices (developing, practising and enacting a beginning repertoire);
>
> » tools (the conceptual/theoretical and practical resources to use);
>
> » dispositions (habits of thinking and action).

(adapted from Hammerness et al, 2005)

More recently Orchard and Winch (2015) have argued for good teaching to be underpinned by the need for practitioners to be able to:

> » understand key educational concepts and the major debates about aims, curriculum and pedagogy that have shaped practice in schools;

» engage with empirical educational research and be capable of assessing its quality and its relevance to their practice;

» think through the ethics of teaching and the challenges of ethical decision-making in the classroom.

(2015, p 5)

The question as to when, and how, beginning teachers acquire such expertise raises a number of critical questions. Do partnerships acknowledge the undoubted demands of teaching and therefore seek to make the process of acquiring basic competence as simple as possible? Within such a model, as exemplified in the Waterside case study, there is not a rejection of research-informed ideas and engagement with theory per se, but more a sense that the trainee teachers do not need to be made explicitly aware of them at this point in time. Practice – extensive experience and regular feedback – takes priority and research-based understandings or theory are seen as coming later, or as being mediated by teachers and vouched for in their practice as something that works, and so can be trusted. Where newly qualified teachers remain within the schools in which they train, or in similar contexts locally, then a programme of well-modelled demonstrations, regular practice and focussed feedback is seen to be effective, but does such a programme equip those teachers to move to other contexts where things may be done differently, or where the specific needs of the learners are very different?

The Carter Review (Carter, 2015) argued that beginning teachers should be taught 'how to evaluate and challenge research findings' (p 23) and to 'interpret educational theory and research in a critical way' (p 8) and we would endorse this claim, but there needs to be clear agreement within partnerships as to when and how such learning takes place. It is not something that should be ignored or treated as being a lesser priority within the overall ITE programme, but rather something that should be addressed as an essential partnership principle.

Principle 4: Roles and responsibilities within the partnership need to be clearly defined and careful consideration given to the way in which responsibility for different aspects of the programme is managed

All those working at different levels within the partnership should make a distinctive contribution to the learning of the beginning teachers in the programme, but the nature of this contribution will vary from role to role. What is important, however, is that different types of expertise are recognised and valued and that collectively they provide an appropriate range of perspectives on which to draw. While what might be considered more traditional models of partnership, involving both universities and school partners working together, would have included such a range of perspectives there is a challenge for schools working in partnership with other schools, within SCITT models, to provide similarly broad perspectives. While school-led partnerships are potentially able to draw on appropriate knowledge and research, particularly with regard to subject-specific pedagogy, there is a question as to which research and theory counts as being useful and which can be accessed relatively easily. The Carter Review argued for the creation of '*a central portal that synthesises the most up to date research findings in different subjects and phases and offers practical summaries to teachers*' (Carter, 2015, p 54) but, even if such a *portal* were to exist, this would not address the issue as to how research is then integrated into the training programme, or how trainee teachers might be taught, as Carter also suggests, '*to challenge and evaluate evidence so that new teachers have the skills to navigate this complex landscape*' (2015, p 53). The Waterside SCITT trainees do have access to an additional programme (enabling them to gain a PGCE with Masters-level credits) but since this is an optional programme delivered in the trainees' own time, and therefore not integrated into their day-to-day training, it may be questionable to what extent it is viewed as relevant to their current needs.

Notwithstanding the many strengths of locating teacher education programmes more fully in the school context, it is important that this training is not wholly focussed on preparing trainees to work in the same, or a similar context to that in which the training is taking place. Those leading training within the partnership therefore need to accept responsibility for providing opportunities for trainees to learn from a range of different perspectives. Even within well-established partnership models the school context can be one where the approach is primarily one of learning by imitation, as with an apprenticeship model, and does not provide sufficient opportunities for trainees to learn either about some of the complexities associated with that specific context or about the complexities that they might encounter in alternative contexts (Douglas, 2011)

Central to the success of any ITE partnership is the contribution of mentors to the learning programme, although it is acknowledged that overall the quality of mentoring is variable, both within partnerships and from one partnership to another (see Chapter 2). While the national standards for school-based mentors in England (DfE, 2016) define clearly the expected characteristics of a mentor and the role in terms of supporting the trainee's teaching and induction into the wider profession, they make no reference to the extent of the mentor's role within the ITE programme itself, for example in relation to the mentor's involvement in the planning of this programme. The requirements of the role at Waterside are set out clearly in the various programme handbooks, in ways that reflect the national standards, with most of the mentor's responsibility seen as residing simply in their day-to-day support of the trainee teacher.

Partnerships may wish to consider, however, how the mentor role might be enhanced, both as a means by which mentors themselves can develop their expertise and also as a way to develop further the learning experiences of the trainees themselves. McIntyre and Hagger (1993) refer to '*developed*' and '*extended*' mentoring (p 94, 100), which goes beyond a minimal level of mentor support and which aims to take full advantage of the mentor's expertise and of the contexts in which the mentor works.

It is therefore clear that the roles of individuals working within any partnership programme need to be carefully defined in order to enable the training programme to draw fully and effectively on the distributed expertise of all those working within it.

Principle 5: Sufficiently high levels of quality assurance need to be in place to ensure consistency, equity and compliance

Quality assurance within partnerships needs to be reflected in a number of different ways. First, all ITE partnerships need to meet the regulatory requirements set out at national level and this requires effective management of the training programme supported by strong administrative systems. There has to be a shared understanding of any statutory frameworks within which training takes place, as well as of the often complex ITE-related funding structures. Second, there needs to be sufficiently rigorous oversight of the programme itself to ensure that quality is maintained at all levels and that trainees are treated equitably and have access to the full range of learning opportunities available to them. Third, there needs to be regular evaluation that focuses on all aspects of the programme and which takes into account programme outcomes, the processes involved and the views of all stakeholders, including those of the trainees themselves. This evaluation should take account of the broader ITE curriculum and its aims, as well as specific elements within it. Such evaluation will also include analysis which draws on a range of programme statistics such as admissions data, data related to the overall performance of specific groups of trainees and relevant outcomes data. Finally, programme developments need to be monitored carefully and evaluated against previously designated anticipated outcome measures.

Conclusions

Partnership working is inherently complex. In order to negotiate its demands, those involved in preparing the next generation of teachers need to engage with the complexity and, through discussion around the nature of the inherent tensions, determine ways of working that best serve the needs of their trainees. In doing so they need to ask a series of critical questions, the answers to which will enable them to develop and strengthen their current provision. These questions include:

»   What are the core aims of our training programme?

»   In what way, if at all, do these distinguish us from other ITE providers?

»   To what extent are all the stakeholders within our partnership involved collaboratively in the planning of our ITE programme?

»   How do the various elements of our programme contribute specifically to the trainees' learning?

»   To what extent is there integration of these different elements and how might such integration be further developed?

»   What opportunities are there for our trainees to draw on and critique a range of different perspectives (including those drawn from both theory and practice)?

» What are our expectations of the trainees at different stages of the training process?

» How are our trainees supported as they engage with the learning programme?

IN A **NUTSHELL**

If partnerships are to work successfully and train their teachers effectively it is important that they consider the nature of the partnership itself, the learning programme offered to the trainees and the roles and responsibilities of all those working to deliver the training programme. We have suggested that five key principles might inform the way in which ITE partnerships might operate:

» Partnerships need to have clear agreement in terms of the programme aims (and specifically a shared view of what the desired trainee outcomes should be).

» Partnerships need a clearly defined *learning* programme in order for their trainee teachers to be able to capitalise fully on their school-based experiences.

» Partnerships need to consider when and how their trainees will develop the adaptive expertise necessary for sustaining a career in teaching.

» Roles and responsibilities within the partnership need to be clearly defined and careful consideration given to the way in which responsibility for different aspects of the programme is managed.

» Sufficiently high levels of quality assurance need to be in place to ensure consistency, equity and compliance.

REFLECTIONS ON **CRITICAL ISSUES**

ITE partnership working invariably creates a certain number of tensions, not least because the training of teachers is not the primary function of the schools in which the majority of such training takes place, but is rather a peripheral activity. Such tensions may be exacerbated when a school is involved in multiple ITE partnerships but may also be reduced significantly if there is no external provider, as is the case with many SCITTs. Tensions can, however, be seen as being creative and enabling, rather than problematic, acknowledging the complexity of partnership working and leading to dialogue between partners as to how best to plan and deliver an effective ITE programme. As Furlong (2006) reminds us, the alternative is that *'professional knowledge becomes simplified, flattened, it is essentially about contemporary practice in schools'* (2006, p 41). Notwithstanding such tensions, it is important that any programme of teacher education is underpinned by key principles that take account of both the needs of the beginning teachers themselves and the complexity of the task which they are undertaking.

REFERENCES

Alexander, R (1984) Innovation and Continuity in the Initial Teacher Education Curriculum, in Alexander, R, Craft, M and Lynch, J (eds) *Change in Teacher Education: Context and Provision since Robins* (pp 103–160). London: Holt, Rinehart and Winston.

Ball, S (2003) The Teacher's Soul and the Terrors of Performativity. *Journal of Education Policy*, 18(2): 215–228.

Bartholomew, S S and Sandholtz, J H (2009) Competing Views of Teaching in a School–University Partnership. *Teaching and Teacher Education*, 25(1): 155–165.

Benton, P (ed) (1990) *The Oxford Internship Scheme: Integration and Partnership in Initial Teacher Education.* London: Calouste Gulbenkian Foundation.

BERA/RSA (2014) *Research and the Teaching Profession: Building the Capacity for a Self-Improving Education System.* London: BERA/RSA.

Berliner, D C (2001) Learning about and Learning from Expert Teachers. *International Journal of Educational Research*, 35(5): 463–482.

Bills, L, Browne, A, Gillespie, H, Gordon, J, Husbands, C, Phillips, E, Still, C and Swatton, P (2008) International Perspectives on Quality in Initial Teacher Education: An Exploratory Review of Selected International Documentation on Statutory Requirements and Quality Assurance, in *Research Evidence in Education Library*. London: EPPI-Centre, Social Science Research Unit, Institute of Education, University of London.

Brisard, E, Menter, I and Smith, I (2005) *Models of Partnership in Programmes of Initial Teacher Education. Full Report of a Systematic Literature Review Commissioned by the General Teaching Council for Scotland.* GTCS Research, Research Publication No. 2. Edinburgh: General Teaching Council for Scotland.

Brown, T, Rowley, H and Smith, K (2015) *The Beginnings of School led Teacher Training: New Challenges for University Teacher Education.* School Direct Research Project Final Report. Manchester Metropolitan University. [online] Available at: www.esri.mmu.ac.uk/resgroups/schooldirect.pdf (accessed 15 May 2018).

Burn, K, Hagger, H and Mutton, T (2015) *Beginning Teachers' Learning: Making Experience Count.* Northwich: Critical Publishing.

Burn, K and Mutton, T (2013) *Review of 'Research-informed Clinical Practice' in Initial Teacher Education.* Research and Teacher Education: The BERA-RSA Inquiry. [online] Available at: www.bera.ac.uk/wp-content/uploads/2014/02/BERA-Paper-4-Research-informed-clinical-practice.pdf (accessed 15 May 2018).

Burton, D (1998) The Changing Role of the University Tutor within School-based Initial Teacher Education: Issues of Role Contingency and Complementarity within a Secondary Partnership. *Journal of Education for Teaching*, 24(2): 129–146.

Carnegie Corporation of New York (2001) *Teachers for a New Era: Transforming Teacher Education.* [online] Available at: http://carnegie.org/fileadmin/Media/Publications/PDF/Carnegie.pdf

Carter, A (2015) *Carter Review of Initial Teacher Training (ITT).* London: DfE. [online] Available at: www.gov.uk/government/publications/carter-review-of-initial-teacher-training (accessed 15 May 2018).

Conroy, J, Hulme, M and Menter, I (2013) Developing a 'Clinical' Model for Teacher Education. *Journal of Education for Teaching: International Research and Pedagogy*, 39(5): 557–573.

Darling-Hammond, L (2006a) *Powerful Teacher Education: Lessons from Exemplary Programs.* San Francisco, CA: Jossey-Bass.

Darling-Hammond, L (2006b) Constructing 21st Century Teacher Education. *Journal of Teacher Education*, 57(3): 300–314.

Darling-Hammond, L (2014) Strengthening Clinical Preparation: The Holy Grail of Teacher Education. *Peabody Journal of Education*, 89(4): 547–561.

Department for Education (DfE) (1992) *Initial Teacher Training (Secondary Phase), Circular 9/92*. London: DfE.

Department for Education (DfE) (1993) *The Initial Training of Primary School Teachers: New Criteria for Course Approval, Circular 16/93*. London: DfE.

Department for Education (DfE) (2010) *The Importance of Teaching. The Schools White Paper 2010*. London: DfE.

Department for Education (DfE) (2011a) *Training Our Next Generation of Outstanding Teachers: An Improvement Strategy for Discussion*. London: DfE. [online] Available at: www.gov.uk/government/publications/training-our-next-generation-of-outstanding-teachers-an-improvement-strategy-for-discussion (accessed 15 May 2018).

Department for Education (DfE) (2011b) *Training Our Next Generation of Outstanding Teachers: Implementation Plan*. London: DfE. [online] Available at: www.gov.uk/government/publications/training-our-next-generation-of-outstanding-teachers-implementation-plan (accessed 15 May 2018).

Department for Education (DfE) (2011c) *Teachers' Standards*. [online] Available at: www.gov.uk/government/uploads/system/uploads/attachment_data/file/301107/Teachers__Standards.pdf (accessed 15 May 2018).

Department for Education (DfE) (2014) *Teaching Schools: A Guide for Potential Applicants*. [online] Available at: www.gov.uk/guidance/teaching-schools-a-guide-for-potential-applicants (accessed 15 May 2018).

Department for Education (DfE) (2016a) *Initial Teacher Training: Government Response to Carter Review*. [online] Available at: www.gov.uk/government/publications/initial-teacher-training-government-response-to-carter-review (accessed 15 May 2018).

Department for Education (DfE) (2016b) *Convert to an Academy: Guide for Schools*. [online] Available at: www.gov.uk/guidance/convert-to-an-academy-information-for-schools-applicants (accessed 15 May 2018).

Department for Education (DfE) and National College for Teaching and Leadership (NCTL) (2017) *Initial Teacher Training: Criteria for Providers*. [online] Available at: www.gov.uk/government/publications/initial-teacher-training-criteria (accessed 15 May 2018).

Department of Education and Science (DES) (1984) *Initial Teacher Training: Approval of Courses* (Circular 3/84). London: DES.

Donaldson, G (2011) *Teaching Scotland's Future: Report of a Review of Teacher Education in Scotland*. Edinburgh, Scotland: Scottish Government.

Douglas, A S (2011) The Different Learning Opportunities Afforded Student Teachers in Four Secondary School Subject Departments in an Initial Teacher Education School–University Partnership in England. *Journal of Education for Teaching*, 37(1): 93–106.

Doyle, W (1977) Learning the Classroom Environment: An Ecological Analysis. *Journal of Teacher Education*, 28(6): 51–55.

Edwards, A and Mutton, T (2007) Looking Forward: Rethinking Professional Learning through Partnership Arrangements in Initial Teacher Education. *Oxford Review of Education*, 33(4): 503–519.

Edwards, A and Protheroe, L (2004) Teaching by Proxy: Understanding How Mentors Are Positioned in Partnerships. *Oxford Review of Education*, 30(2): 183–197.

Everton, T and White, S (1992) Partnership in Training: The University of Leicester's New Model of School-based Teacher Education. *Cambridge Journal of Education*, 22(2): 143–155.

Furlong, J (2013) *Education – An Anatomy of the Discipline: Rescuing the University Project?* London: Routledge.

Furlong, J (2015) Teaching Tomorrow's Teachers. Options for the Future of Initial Teacher Education in Wales. [online] Available at: http://gov.wales/docs/dcells/publications/150309-teaching-tomorrows-teachers-final.pdf

Furlong, J, Barton, L, Miles, S, Whiting, C and Whitty, G (2000) *Teacher Education in Transition: Reforming Professionalism.* Buckingham: Open University Press.

Furlong, J, Campbell, A, Howson, J, Lewis, S and McNamara, O (2006) Partnership in English Initial Teacher Education: Changing Times, Changing Definitions. Evidence from the Teacher Training Agency's National Partnership Project. *Scottish Educational Review*, 37: 32–45.

Furlong, J, McNamara, O, Campbell, A, Howson, J and Lewis, S (2008) Partnership, Policy and Politics: Initial Teacher Education in England. *Teachers and Teaching: Theory and Practice*, 14(4): 307–318.

Furlong, J, Whitty, G, Whiting, C, Miles, S, Barton, L and Barrett, E (1996) Re-defining Partnership: Revolution or Reform in Initial Teacher Education? *Journal of Education for Teaching: International Research and Pedagogy*, 22(1): 39–56.

Gove, M (2010) Speech to the National College Annual Conference. [online] Available at: www.gov.uk/government/speeches/michael-gove-to-the-national-college-annual-conference-birmingham (accessed 15 May 2018).

Griffiths, V and Owen, P (eds) (1995) *Schools in Partnership.* London: Paul Chapman.

Hagger, H, Burn, K, Mutton, T and Brindley, S (2008) Practice Makes Perfect? Learning to Learn as a Teacher. *Oxford Review of Education*, 34(2): 159–178.

Hagger, H and McIntyre, D (2006) *Learning Teaching from Teachers: Realizing the Potential of School-based Teacher Education.* Maidenhead: Open University Press.

Hallinan, M T and Khmelkov, V T (2001) Recent Developments in Teacher Education in the United States of America. *Journal of Education for Teaching: International Research and Pedagogy*, 27(2): 175–185.

Hammerness, K (2006) From Coherence in Theory to Coherence in Practice. *Teachers College Record*, 108(7): 1241–1265.

Hammerness, K, Darling-Hammond, L and Bransford, J with Berliner, D, Cochran-Smith, M, McDonald, M and Zeichner, K (2005) How Teachers Learn and Develop, in Darling-Hammond, L and Bransford, J with LePage, P, Hammerness, K and Duffy, H (eds) *Preparing Teachers for a Changing World: What Teachers Should Learn and Be Able to Do.* San Francisco, CA: Jossey-Bass.

Hammerness, K, van Tartwijk, J and Snoek, M (2012) Teacher Preparation in the Netherlands, in Darling-Hammond, L and Lieberman, A (eds) *Teacher Education around the World: Changing Policies and Practices.* Abingdon: Routledge.

Hobson, A J, Ashby, P, Malderez, A and Tomlinson, P D (2009) Mentoring Beginning Teachers: What We Know and What We Don't. *Teaching and Teacher Education*, 25(1): 207–216.

Holmes Group (1986) *Tomorrow's Teachers: A Report of the Holmes Group.* East Lansing, MI: The Holmes Group.

Jones, M and Straker, K (2006) What Informs Mentors' Practice When Working with Trainees and Newly Qualified Teachers? An Investigation into Mentors' Professional Knowledge Base. *Journal of Education for Teaching*, 32(2): 165–184.

Kriewaldt, J and Turnidge, D (2013) Conceptualising an Approach to Clinical Reasoning in the Education Profession. *Australian Journal of Teacher Education*, 38(6): 103–115.

Livingston, K and Shiach, L (2010) Co-constructing a New Model of Teacher Education, in Campbell, A and Groundwater-Smith, S (eds) *Connecting Inquiry and Professional Learning in Education: International Perspectives and Practical Solutions.* Abingdon: Routledge.

Mattsson, M, Eilertson, T and Rorrison, D (eds) (2011) *A Practicum Turn in Teacher Education*. Rotterdam: Sense.

McIntyre, D (1990) Ideas and Principles Guiding the Internship Scheme, in Benton, P (ed) *The Oxford Internship Scheme: Integration and partnership in Initial Teacher Education*. London: Calouste Gulbenkian.

McIntyre, D (1993) Theory, Theorizing and Reflection, in Calderhead, J and Gates, P (eds) *Conceptualizing Reflection in Teacher Education*. London: Falmer Press.

McIntyre, D (1997) A Research Agenda for Initial Teacher Education, in McIntyre, D (ed) *Teacher Education Research in a New Context* (pp 1–5). London: Paul Chapman.

McIntyre, D (2009) The Difficulties of Inclusive Pedagogy for Initial Teacher Education and Some Thoughts on the Way Forward. *Teaching and Teaching Education*, 25(4): 602–608.

McIntyre, D and Hagger, H (1993) Teachers' Expertise and Models of Mentoring, in McIntyre, D, Hagger, H and Wilkin, M (eds) *Mentoring: Perspectives on School-based Teacher Education* (pp 86–102). London: Kogan Page.

McLean Davies, L, Anderson, M, Deans, J, Dinham, S, Griffin, P, Kameniar, B, Page, J, Reid, C, Rickards, F, Tayler, C and Tyler, D (2013) Masterly Preparation: Embedding Clinical Practice in a Graduate Pre-service Teacher Education Programme. *Journal of Education for Teaching: International Research and Pedagogy*, 39(1): 93–106.

McNamara, O and Murray, J (2013) *The School Direct Programme and Its Implications for Research-Informed Teacher Education and Teacher Educators*. York: Higher Education Academy.

Murray, J and Mutton, T (2015) Teacher Education in England; Change in Abundance, Continuities in Question, in Teacher Education Group (Beauchamp et al). *Teacher Education in Times of Change*. Bristol: Policy Press.

Mutton, T (2016) Partnership in Teacher Education, in Teacher Education Group (Beauchamp et al). *Teacher Education in Times of Change*. Bristol: Policy Press.

Mutton, T and and Butcher, J (2008) 'We Will Take Them from Anywhere': Schools Working within Multiple Initial Teacher Training Partnerships. *Journal of Education for Teaching: International Research and Pedagogy*, 34(1): 45–62.

Office for Standards in Education (Ofsted) (2015) Initial Teacher Education Inspection Handbook. [online] Available at: www.gov.uk/government/publications/initial-teacher-education-inspection-handbook (accessed 15 May 2018).

Organisation for Economic Co-operation and Development (OECD) (2005) *Teachers Matter: Attracting, Developing and Retaining Effective Teachers*. Paris: OECD Publishing.

Organisation for Economic Co-operation and Development (OECD) (2007) *Improving the Quality of Teacher Education*. Paris: OECD Publishing.

Pendry, A (1997) The Pedagogical Thinking and Learning of History Teachers, in McIntyre, D (ed) *Teacher Education Research in a New Context: The Oxford Internship Scheme*. London: Paul Chapman Publishing.

Sahlberg, P (2012) The Most Wanted: Teachers and Teacher Education in Finland, in Darling-Hammond, L and Lieberman, A (eds) *Teacher Education around the World: Changing Policies and Practices*. Abingdon: Routledge.

Sahlberg, P, Broadfoot, P, Coolahan, J, Furlong, J and Kirk, G (2014) *Aspiring to Excellence. Final Report of the International Review Panel on the Structure of Initial Teacher Education in Northern Ireland*. [online] Available at: www.delni.gov.uk/aspiring-to-excellence-review-panel-final-report.pdf (accessed 15 May 2018).

Schleicher, A (2011) *Building a High-Quality Teaching Profession: Lessons from around the World*. Paris: OECD Publishing.

Smedley, L (2001) Impediments to Partnership: A Literature Review of School–University Links. *Teachers and Teaching: Theory and Practice*, 7(2): 189–209.

Tatto, M (1996) Examining Values and Beliefs about Teaching Diverse Students: Understanding the Challenges for Teacher Education. *Educational Evaluation and Policy Analysis*, 18: 155–180.

Tatto, M T, Burn, K, Menter, I, Mutton, T and Thompson, I (2018) *Learning to Teach in England and the United States: The Evolution of Policy and Practice*. London: Routledge.

Taylor, A (2008) Developing Understanding about Learning to Teach in a University–Schools Partnership. *British Educational Research Journal*, 31(1): 63–90.

Teacher Education Group (2016) *Teacher Education in Times of Change*. Bristol: Policy Press.

Teitel, L (1998) Professional Development Schools: A Literature Review, in Levine, M (ed) *Designing Standards that Work for Professional Development Schools*. Washington, DC: National Council for Accreditation of Teacher Education.

Universities UK (2014) *The Impact of Initial Teacher Training Reforms on English Higher Education Institutions*. [online] Available at: www.universitiesuk.ac.uk/highereducation/Pages/ImpactOfITTreforms.aspx#.VKz7SE0qVdg (accessed 15 May 2018).

Winch, C, Oancea, A and Orchard, J (2015) The Contribution of Educational Research to Teachers' Professional Learning: Philosophical Understandings. *Oxford Review of Education*, 41(2): 202–216.

Zeichner, K (2009) *Teacher Education and the Struggle for Social Justice*. New York: Routledge.

Zeichner, K (2010) Rethinking the Connections between Campus Courses and Field Experiences in College-and University-based Teacher Education. *Journal of Teacher Education*, 61(1–2): 89–99.

Zeichner, K and Bier, M (2014) The Turn toward Practice and Clinical Experience in US Teacher Education, in Arnold, K-H, Gröschner, A and Hascher, T (eds) *Schulpraktika in der Lehrbildung. Theoretische Grundlagen, Konzeptionen, Prozesse und Effekte*. Münster: Waxmann.

INDEX